POUND AS WUZ

ESSAYS AND LECTURES ON EZRA POUND

1 9 8 7

OTHER BOOKS BY JAMES LAUGHLIN

James Laughlin: Selected Poems 1935–1985 (1986)

The Master of Those Who Know: Pound the Teacher (1986)

New Directions Annuals: 1–50 *ff* (Editor, 1937 to present)

The House of Light (poetry, 1986)

The Owl of Minerva (poetry, 1987)

Stolen and Contaminated Poems (1985)

P O U N D

A S   W U Z

Essays and Lectures

on Ezra Pound

by James Laughlin

GRAYWOLF PRESS : SAINT PAUL

Library of Congress Cataloging-in-Publication Data

Laughlin, James, 1914–
    Pound as wuz.

    Bibliography: p.
    Includes index.
    1. Pound, Ezra, 1885–1972. 2. Poets, American—
20th century—Biography. I. Title.
PS3531.082Z728 1987   811'.52 [B]   87-81376
ISBN 1-55597-097-4
ISBN 1-55597-098-2 (pbk.)

Acknowledgments

"Ez as Wuz" was a lecture given at the Ezra Pound Centennial Colloquium, San Jose State University, and was first published in *San Jose Studies*.

"Pound's Pedagogy" was delivered at the Centennial Observance for Ezra Pound at Yale University and was first published as a book with the title *The Master of Those Who Know* by City Lights Books, San Francisco.

Text of Pound's story "In the Water-Butt" courtesy of The Beinecke Library and Rare Book Room, Yale University; it was first published as a part of "Walking Around a Water-Butt" in *The Paris Review* (Copyright © 1986 by the Trustees of the Ezra Pound Literary Property Trust).

Parts of "Motz el Son" first appeared as the introduction to Pound's *Forked Branches: Translations of Medieval Poems*, published by The Windhover Press at the University of Iowa. Part also appeared in *Antaeus*.

"Rambling Around Pound's *Propertius*" was first published in *Field*.

An earlier version of "An Introduction to the *Cantos*" was published in *The New York Times Book Review*.

"Some Voices from Canto 74" was a lecture delivered in English 150 at Brown University.

"Pound's Economics" was a lecture delivered at the Ezra Pound Symposium at the University of Alabama, and first published in *Ezra Pound: 1885–1972: The Legacy of Kulchur* (Tuscaloosa: The University of Alabama Press).

"E.P.: The Lighter Side" was a lecture given at the Ezra Pound Centennial Colloquium at the University of Maine, Orono.

Some pages from various of the above pieces were first published by *American Poetry*.

Grateful acknowledgment is made to New Directions Publishing Corp. for permission to quote from the following copyrighted works of Ezra Pound: *The ABC of Reading* (Copyright © 1934 by Ezra Pound); *The Cantos* (Copyright © 1934, 1937, 1940, 1948, 1950, 1956, 1959, 1962, 1963, 1965, 1966, 1968, 1970, 1971 by Ezra Pound; Copyright © 1969, 1972 by the Estate of Ezra Pound; Copyright © 1973, 1986 by the Trustees of the Ezra Pound Literary Property Trust); *The Classic Noh Theatre of Japan* (Copyright © 1959 by New Directions Publishing Corp.); *Collected Early Poems* (Copyright © 1976 by the Trustees of the Ezra Pound Literary Property Trust); *Guide to Kulchur* (Copyright © 1970 by Ezra Pound; all rights reserved); "Hilda's Book" in *End to Torment* by H. D. (Copyright © 1979 by the Trustees of the Ezra Pound Literary Property Trust); *Pavannes and Divagations* (Copyright © 1958 by Ezra Pound); *Personae* (Copyright © 1926 by Ezra Pound); *The Spirit of Romance* (Copyright © 1968 by Ezra Pound); *Translations* (Copyright © 1954, 1963 by Ezra Pound; all rights reserved). Previously unpublished material by Ezra Pound, Copyright © 1987 by the Trustees of the Ezra Pound Literary Property Trust; used by permission of New Directions Publishing Corp., agents.

Grateful acknowledgment is also given to New Directions Publishing Corp. for permission to quote from William Carlos Williams' *Paterson* (Copyright © 1946, 1948, 1949, 1951, 1958 by William Carlos Williams). Previously unpublished material by William Carlos Williams, Copyright © 1987 by William Eric Williams and Paul H. Williams; used by permission of New Directions Publishing Corp., agents.

Grateful acknowledgment is also given to The Windhover Press for permission to quote from *Forked Branches: Translation of Medieval Poems* (Copyright © 1985 by the Trustees of the Ezra Pound Literary Property Trust).

Previously unpublished quotes from postcards written by Dorothy Shakespear Pound, Copyright © 1987 by Omar Pound: used by permission of Omar Pound.

The author is indebted to Dean Sheridan and the Faculty of English who permitted him to give seminars on Pound and Williams at Brown University, and to two friends at the Beinecke Library at Yale: Christa Sammons, who edited this book, and Donald Gallup, Pound's bibliographer, who over the years has given the author so much information and encouragement.

Publication of this book is made possible in part by donations to Graywolf Press from The Bush Foundation, The National Endowment for the Arts, and contributors to United Arts, of which Graywolf is a member organization.

Published by GRAYWOLF PRESS
Post Office Box 75006
Saint Paul, MN 55175

FOR MARY DE RACHEWILTZ

CONTENTS

ILLUSTRATIONS

THE JAZZ OF JAZ

by Hugh Kenner

Without him, what literature would America have to show for this century? So much is chance. Writers write, little presses spew out paper, and who sees any of it, or cares? The book trade, that's where the bucks are; by reiteration, where the names are.

James Laughlin—"Jaz" to Ezra Pound—kept every book of Pound's in print, whether they sold or no; and kept everything by William Carlos Williams in print, whether it sold or no; until it all began to sell, years slowly yielding readers, a few passing word to more; and now the Modernist Canon—this is irrefutable—contains, among a very few names, Pound and Williams.

Because of their talents? Yes, of course. But thanks to Jaz also, who kept them from going the way of William Blake—a little-press author (Blake was his own press)—who got put into circulation, by W. B. Yeats, only when he'd been dead sixty-five years. No tradition of reading Blake extends from his own time, not the way the tradition of reading "The Waste Land" extends from 1922. That it's a twenties poem, that the twenties received it, is part of its meaning now. But, feeling our way back to Blake, we reach only the 1890s. We can't place him in his own time: can't conceive him there. So with all respect, we stay unsure what to make of him. And how easily a like fate could have cordoned off Pound and Williams! Published by little presses that went out of business, they might have been curiosities for 2035 to be struck by.

Jaz a half-century ago went straight to the root: put what you respect in print, and keep it available. Góing to the root is part of his temperament, and his mentor at the Ezuversity reinforced it.

Which brings us to this book, the longest, fullest, most devoted picture of Ezra Pound in his great days that we are likely to have. The Pound I first met in 1948 was a prisoner who'd been through something resembling shell-shock. Spontaneities, genialities, had been partly stunned. But the Pound James Laughlin had known a dozen years earlier—! Well, read about him.

His great days? His great creative period, pre-Pisa, had been the late London years and the Paris ones: the years of *Propertius*, of *Mauberley*, of 30 *Cantos*. By the mid-thirties a sense of responsibility for human events was pushing the Puritan didact toward the surface, and the impulse to hang fiscal witches. Still, Laughlin's Pound was gestating the *Guide to Kulchur*, something with a scope he'd not have envisaged in 1925, and with the old good humor still active. To learn about the world and history, not just about verse-craft, Laughlin came in at exactly the right moment.

And what a writer Laughlin is! If he can relive and make us share his juvenescent naivetés, it's not because they aren't long outgrown but because he seems unhampered by self-importance. Unencumbered, even, by any awareness of being a less limited poet than e. e. cummings, he doesn't even publish himself. An unassuming performer, he'll let you think he aspires to no more than kitten-on-the-keys. Verse or prose, though, it's first-rate jazz.

POUND AS WUZ

EZ AS WUZ

I may be the last survivor who knew Pound in his best years, in his prime. Perhaps I can report what he was like before the newspapers turned him into a monster. I'd like to tell a little about Ezra and Rapallo in 1934–35 when I was studying in his "Ezuversity." Then something about publishing him and how he endured the years in St. Elizabeths. Finally some recollections of his sad old age.

The best thing that ever happened to me for my education was that my master at Choate, Dudley Fitts, started me reading Pound. He had been corresponding with Pound about the affairs of Lincoln Kirstein's *Hound & Horn* magazine, to which Pound always referred as the "Bitch and Bugle." We also read T. S. Eliot and Gertrude Stein—remarkable for a prep school. As I was bored my first terms at Harvard, which was just then between two generations of great professors, Fitts arranged for me to go to Europe, to Rapallo, to study with Pound in his famous Ezuversity for several months. James Joyce once described Pound as "a large bundle of unpredictable electricity," which certainly was apt for when I knew him in Rapallo.

The Ezuversity was an ideal institution for a twentieth-century goliard. First of all, there was no tuition. Ezra was always hard up, but he wouldn't take any payment. The only expenses I had were renting a room and paying for my meals with Mrs. Pound and him at the Albergo Rapallo, which he called the "Albuggero Rapallo." The reason they ate in the Albergo was that Dorothy Pound, a most lovable woman, was a lady from Kensington and she had never been taught to cook. The classes usually met at the lunch table. They might begin with Ezra going through the day's mail, commenting on the subjects that it raised. He had a huge correspondence from all over the world; he told me that postage was his largest expense. Economics, of course, was by then his major concern; but there were letters from writers and translators, from professors and scholars of Chinese and the Renaissance, from monetary theorists, from artists, letters from Eliot, from Jean Cocteau, and, of course, from Ernest Hemingway. Pound and Hemingway were devoted friends but Pound confided in me, "the trouble with Hem is that he can't keep two ideas in his head at the same time."

Many interesting things came out of Pound's mail. I remember one day at lunch Ezra tossed a paperback across the table to me, saying, "Waal, Jaz, here's a dirty book that's pretty good." It was Henry Miller's *Tropic of Cancer*. Whence came my friendship with Henry that lasted till his death. To be sure, I was never able to publish *Tropic of Cancer* in the States because I knew my family would disinherit me; but New Directions did about twenty of Henry's less startling books, most of them collections of essays and stories.

The Course of Study

After he had covered the mail, Pound would get on to the real subjects of the course. These were literature and history the way he wanted to revise it, because of course, as he insisted, all history has been miswritten since Gibbon. And poetics and the interpretation of culture. All this information was delivered in the colloquial. Ez always spoke in the colloquial. That was the tone of his discourse. I remember one day he said that it didn't matter where "Fat-faced Frankie," by whom he meant Francesco Petrarch, placed all those adjectives in his lines. They were just for decoration, not sense.

Pound was a superb mimic and had total recall. He used five different accents. He had an American cracker-barrel accent, an

Ezra Pound around 1938. This photo was used as a publicity shot by New Directions for years.

American Black accent, he had cockney, he had bistro French, but my favorite was the "Oirrish" of Uncle Willie Yeats.

Most astonishing was his word play. Aristotle was "Harry Stottle," and Aristophanes was "Harry-Stop-Her-Knees." Every class was a performance by an actor with many personae; his hamming was part of his pedagogy. Equally exciting were the marginalia in the books from his personal library, which he lent me to study. The most frequent comment in the margins of his

Herodotus was "Balls!!!" I read Propertius in his Mueller edition with his underlinings of passages to be used in the *Homage to Sextus Propertius*. In his de Mailla's *Histoire Générale de la Chine*, I found checked the emperors he had chosen for the Chinese Cantos, with a big star beside Emperor Tching Tang, who had the characters for "Make It New" engraved on his bathtub.

The Ezuversity was peripatetic. Ezra was not didactic on the tennis court because he was usually too out of breath. But when he rowed out into the beautiful Tigullian Gulf in a *patino* to swim, the flow of useful knowledge continued. I remember especially one day when we were walking up one of the *salite*, the steep stony paths behind Rapallo. Ezra had brought along a packet of scraps from the lunch table to feed the cats that were waiting for him on top of the stone walls of the little hillside farms. "Micci-micci-micci, vieni qua c'è da mangiare." (Come kitty, come kitty, here's something to eat.) As we walked he explained the Eleusinian Mysteries, about *dromena* and *epopte*, and went on to the bizarre theories you will find in the postscript to his translation of De Gourmont's *Physique de l'amour*.

Another day when we were walking up toward San Ambrogio we got onto the subject of what he would do with his Nobel prize money when he won it. He decided that he would get a very good cook so that he wouldn't have to eat any longer in the Albuggero Rapallo. Well, of course he never did win it, which was a blow.

In the evenings he loved to go to the movies. In those days, art had not yet reached the Italian cinema. These were the worst movies ever, absolutely inane comedies. But Ezra would sit up in the balcony with his feet on the railing, wearing his cowboy hat, eating popcorn, and roaring with laughter. They were terrible films, but they helped me learn some Italian.

The room where Ezra worked—the Pounds had a small but beautiful penthouse apartment in one of the old buildings on the seafront—was interesting. He had it well organized. So that he could easily find them, he hung his glasses and his extra glasses, his pencils, his pens, his scissors, and his stapler on strings from the ceiling over his desk. I watched him working sometimes. He would assault his typewriter with an incredible vigor. In fact, he had to have two typewriters, because one was always at the repair shop. His typing, which was extremely eccentric, had, I think, a good deal to do with the visual arrangement of some of the pages in the *Cantos* because, in the fury of composition, he couldn't always take time to go all the way back to the left margin; he would slap the carriage and wherever it stopped that determined the indent.

What Not to Do

Pound saved me some grief by pointing out that I shouldn't waste time trying to write fiction, for Flaubert, Stendhal, Henry James, Ford Madox Ford, and Joyce had done everything with fiction that could be done. No one else should bother. But I was still trying very hard to write poetry. The results were awful — copies of Pound without his virtues. Ezra would take his pencil and slash away, with "No, no, that won't do! You don't need that word. That's slop!" Finally, near the time of my departure, he took me aside and said, "No, Jaz, it's hopeless. You're never gonna make a writer. No matter how hard you try, you'll never make it. I want you to go back to Amurrica and do something useful."

"Waaal, Boss, what's useful?"

He thought a moment and suggested, "Waaal, you might assassernate Henry Seidel Canby." [1]

But we agreed I wasn't smart enough to get away with it. For a second choice he suggested, "Go back and be a publisher. Go back to Haavud to finish up your studies. If you're a good boy, your parents will give you some money and you can bring out books. I'll write to my friends and get them to provide you with manuscripts."

And that's how it happened. I went back to Haavud and began printing books. I've never regretted obeying his edict. But poetry is hard to suppress. Some ten years later, encouraged by William Carlos Williams, I began to write light verse — and have had much enjoyment from it.

I observed Pound's Chinese studies. Most days after lunch he would go up to his bedroom to take off into China. Curiosity about China came into Pound's head as a boy. Back in Wyncote, Pennsylvania, his parents supported Chinese missions and showed him books about China. Lying on the bed, in Rapallo, his big black hat shading his eyes, he would prop a huge Chinese dictionary on a pillow on his stomach. He had been drawn to Chinese in 1913 by the notebooks of Ernest Fenollosa, an extraordinary linguist but one who apparently had not cottoned to the fact that not all of the Chinese characters are ideoglyphic. There, then, was Ezra lying on his bed, looking for the pictures of things or people or signs that he thought should be in the characters. Often they weren't, and he couldn't reconcile what he saw in the characters with the dictionary meanings. As a result he invented meanings of his own. Sinologists deplore these inventions. But for most of us his language and his lines are so beautiful that the inaccuracies hardly matter. Eliot said that Pound invented Chinese poetry for our time.

The *Cantos* were written, as far as I could see and I sometimes watched him at work, entirely from memory—more aural than visual memory. I saw no three-by-five cards in his workroom. All that vast store of information was in his head. Composing a canto he would put down what he remembered, usually accurately, but he seldom checked. If you consult Carroll F. Terrell's exhaustive *Companion to the Cantos*, which tracks down every reference, you will find recorded quite a number of incorrect spellings and confusions in quotations or in paraphrases from sources.

When, at New Directions, we were publishing the successive volumes of the *Cantos*, scholars would point out bad spellings and we corrected them. There were about six hundred such corrections. Then at a certain point, Hugh Kenner said, "Look, fellows, we'd better stop correcting, because we may be spoiling some of his best puns."

Pound's Greek was a problem. He knew Greek but he didn't worry much about the accents. We used to send those passages to Dudley Fitts to clean up.

A postcard of Rapallo.

Why Rapallo?

Why Rapallo for his home? people often ask. There was an argument about that at the Yale Pound Conference in 1985. Why did he move from Paris to Rapallo? The learned Poundians gave abstruse psychological theories to explain the choice. But it's really very simple. Ezra told me, "I came here because I like the swimming." During the years when he was based in London and Paris, he made many visits to Italy. He lived in Venice as early as 1908. He loved Verona and Sirmio, but he chose Rapallo over such more glamorous places because the trains from Paris to Rome all stop in Rapallo. Friends and admirers dropped off to see him. The Ezuversity flourished because Rapallo was easy to reach. And Rapallo is a beautiful spot. On the Tigullian Gulf—one of the bays on the Ligurian coast below Genoa—it has lovely mountains rising from the sea with umbrella pines on them. It has an old *castello* built out into the water. There is the sound of the church bells at four o'clock ringing down into the town from a dozen little villages on the mountainside.

Pound loved Rapallo and the Rapallesi loved him. They remembered him with affection, as I found when I went back a few years ago to work on a documentary film about him. They harbored no resentment about his pro-fascist leanings. The newspaper editor explained, "Noi siamo tutti stati fascisti." (We were all fascists!)

Pound's father, Homer, worked most of his life in the Philadelphia mint. Ezra, an only child, was always a dutiful son. When Homer retired, Ezra brought his parents to live in Rapallo. In the Beinecke Library at Yale there are more than eight hundred letters that Ezra wrote to Homer and Isabel.

The old folks, as Pound called them and as I called them, lived up the hill in a villa that Yeats had once rented. Their social life was restricted because they couldn't learn Italian. Their life revolved around Ezra. Homer called him "son," but Isabel favored "Ra," his boyhood nickname. Homer was naive, unsophisticated, sweet, and lovable—a very American old man. But Isabel was somewhat upper class in her manner. She was, after all, a New England Wadsworth, related to Henry Wadsworth Longfellow. I remember her as being fluttery. She had brought her china from home and liked to give tea parties, but since she didn't know many people, there were few guests.

Isabel was the one who had pushed Ezra since his childhood to be a poet. She encouraged him to read and to write. What, of course, Isabel really wanted was to be the mother of a poet. But with their background neither Isabel nor Homer could understand much of "son's" work, especially after he began the *Cantos*. It was simply beyond them, this complicated, polylingual poetry. When I went up the hill to call on them, they would quiz me on what "son" or "Ra" was doing and what it meant. I'm afraid I wasn't too helpful. But they were very sweet people.

Italian Nobility

Rapallo was a town of petits bourgeois and retired people, among them a good many English who did not find Ezra congenial. But there was also a very small segment of the Italian nobility—the San Faustinos, the Robilantes, and the Collis. Ezra was a darling of these people. He amused them. The gentry met at noon in a little closed café in a back street—they wouldn't go to the tourist cafés on the seafront. Ezra often went there at noon, though he almost never drank anything. They made much of him and he loved it.

There wasn't much literary life in Rapallo. For that Pound was dependent on people who came through the Ezuversity, such as, among the most famous, the poets Louis Zukofsky and Basil Bunting. Max Beerbohm, the great British writer-cartoonist, had a villa in Rapallo, but Pound seldom saw him. There was Monti, the painter who did the much reproduced portrait of Ezra walking along the sea wall. There was John Drummond, a young Englishman who became a kind of public relations assistant for Pound, writing letters on economic subjects to the London newspapers, which were seldom printed.

There was a group around the local paper, *Il Mare*, in which Pound instigated a cultural section. There were tennis friends at the club such as the charming Dr. Bacigalupo. Ezra was an enthusiastic tennis player; he had a forehand drive, executed with a 90-degree body pivot, which none of us could return. He organized a series of concerts held in the town hall of Rapallo.

Pound playing tennis at Rapallo.

The concerts featured his favorite composers—Bach, Mozart, and Vivaldi. The nucleus of the performers was Olga Rudge, Ezra's friend from 1920 until his death and an accomplished concert violinist, and the German pianist, Gerhardt Munch, who lived in Rapallo. Guest stars were imported from time to time.

After literature, Chinese, and economic reform, music was Pound's great passion. This preoccupation grew out of his long study and translation of the Provençal troubadour poets. From them he took the concept of *motz el son*, that poetry is song and that words must be equated with verbal sounds. He never had formal musical training but he heard much music in his London years when he wrote music criticism for the *New Age* under the pseudonym of "William Atheling." He bought a clavichord from Arnold Dolmetsch, the reviver of ancient music. On this instrument he tapped out with one finger the melodic lines for his two short operas, *Le Testament*, with words by François Villon, and *Cavalcanti*, using texts from Dante's friend, Guido Cavalcanti. These scores are monodic—what interested Pound was the duration in music of the vowel sounds in the poetry— with orchestration supplied by his friends George Antheil and Agnes Bedford. At first neglected, these operas have been performed here and abroad several times. They are unusual and engaging music.

An anecdote will illustrate Ezra's taste in music. One of the best trips I ever made with Olga and him was to visit the town of Wörgl in Austria. Wörgl is one of two places on record where Silvio Gesell's stampscrip—one of Pound's favorite panaceas for monetary reform—was ever systematically tried out. It worked for a time; then the central bank in Vienna found out about it and that was the end of that. From Wörgl we went on to Salzburg to the music festival. Ezra loved Mozart, but I made the mistake of taking him one night to the *Festspielhaus*, where Toscanini was conducting Beethoven's *Fidelio*. After about fifteen minutes, Ezra reared up in his seat and expostulated quite loudly, "What can you expect? The man had syphilis." We trooped out; Toscanini didn't miss a beat.

Distressing Topic

Pound's anti-Semitism is a distressing topic.[2] It did much to ruin his life. It was the one thing I didn't like at the Ezuversity, though at that time it was limited to jokes and attacks on bankers such as the Rothschilds and Sir Montagu Norman of the Bank of England. When I challenged him about it, he simply said, "How can a man whose name is Ezra be anti-Semitic?" Pound's friendships with the poets Louis Zukofsky and Allen Ginsberg are recorded. But I'd like to speak of his kindness to the Jewish sculptor, Henghes, whose real name was Heinz Winterfeld Klussmann.

One day when I was in Rapallo, a bedraggled figure with his feet bleeding turned up on Ezra's doorstep. In Hamburg he had heard that Ezra had some sculptures by Henri Gaudier-Brzeska, a friend of Pound's from the London days. Henghes wanted to see them and get advice from Ezra about his own work. He had no money, so he had walked most of the way from Germany. In the mountains he had picked up in a stream bed some small pieces of soft slate and then carved them with his pocketknife. The minute Ezra saw these pieces he knew Henghes was good and wanted to help him, as he had helped artists and writers all his life. There was no extra bed in the apartment, so he put Henghes up in the large dog kennel on the terrace. He fed him and, as soon as Henghes was rested up a bit, took him over to the local stonecutter, the man who carved the gravestones. Pound said, "I will stand good for a piece of stone for this man and you lend him some tools." Henghes went to work carving the striking figure of a centaur, which later became the model for the New Directions book colophon. People do say from time to time that it is a sitting-down horse, but why shouldn't a centaur rest? Then Ezra went up to Turin with a photograph of the statue to show to the wife of the head of the Fiat Company, Signora Agnelli. He convinced her that Henghes had genius and she bought the statue for a good price.

Henghes was able to move out of the dog kennel and pursue his art and the young ladies of Rapallo. He went on to a consid-

New Directions colophon from model by Henghes.

erable success. His greatest fame came when he had moved to London and was commissioned to do a statue for the middle of a pool at the new Festival Hall across the Thames. This statue, a seated figure of a man, caught the fancy of the youth of London. Every night someone would wade into the pond to put a different funny hat on the figure. The tabloids began running pictures that made Henghes so famous he was asked to do a piece for the Time-Life Building. The importance of publicity. But Ezra started it.

Some Poundians try to brush Ezra's anti-Semitism under the rug. That is foolish. It is there and we have to face it and think about it. There are, to be sure, a few overtly anti-Semitic lines in the *Cantos*, but the wartime broadcasts that he made from Rome Radio are virulent. As Alfred Kazin said, "They show a mind in trouble." In them, Pound called FDR "the Jew Rosenfeld." Like that—and more. At the same time, many of the broadcasts deal with literary and cultural topics and show him as his old self—a great and witty critic—the way he was before the obsession with economic reform took over.

When Pound was awarded the Bollingen Prize for the *Pisan Cantos*, his critics asked, "Can a bad man write a good poem?" I think that many good poems have been written by unsavory characters. The question is an over-simplification, but we must try to answer it.

Some years after Rapallo, when I had become Pound's publisher, I pressed him again about the anti-Semitism. This is what he answered:

Again in Cantos all institutions are judged on their merits, idem religions. No one can be boosted or exempted on grounds of being a Lutheran or a Manichean, nor can all philosophy be degraded to status of propaganda merely because the author has one philosophy and not another. Is the *Divina Comedia* propaganda or not? From 72 on we will enter the Empyrean, philosophy, George Santayana, etc. [He is referring to when he gets to Canto 72.] The pub'r cannot expect to control the religion and philosophy of his authors. Certain evil habits of language, etc. must be weighed and probably will be found wanting. I shall not accept the specific word anti-Semitism. There will have to be a general formula covering Mennonites, Mohammedans, Lutherans, Calvinists. I wouldn't swear to not being anti-Calvinist, but that don't mean I should weigh protestants in one balance and Anglocats in another. All ideas coming from the near-east are probably shit. If they turn out to be typhus in the laboratory, so is it. So is Taoism, so is probably all Chinese philosophy and religion except Kung [he means Confucius]. I am not yet sure.

Pound's extreme anti-Semitism in the 1940s put a severe strain on my affection for him. But I came to understand his obsession with more charity when Dr. Overholser, the head psychiatrist at St. Elizabeths Hospital, told me, "You mustn't judge Pound morally, you must judge him medically." He explained that Ezra was paranoid and that anti-Semitism is a recognized element in paranoia. Pound could not control himself.

Publishing Pound

It was a pleasure to publish Pound. Some writers complain a lot. But if Pound was annoyed about something, he would fuss for only one letter, in the next he would have forgotten it. He had a reputation for irascibility, but that was mostly when he was writing to or about Nicholas Murray Butler, the president of Columbia, whom he considered the greatest cultural criminal in the United States, or to Sir Montagu Norman. With me he was indulgent and put up with my lapses. Well, he did get quite angry when I printed two of his Chinese characters upside down. But he didn't demand that the page be reprinted. Another ghastly mistake I made was in one of the volumes of the *Cantos*. My knowledge of American history is very slight, and on the back flap of the book I had written "J. Quincy Adams" instead of "John Adams." What an explosion!

> Do you realize that if a man weren't already in bughouse, to read J. Quincy Adams on cover when it should be John Adams père not fils is enough to put a man there. Really there is no known language to express BALLS . . . Oh hell you went to Haavud.

And finally a complaint about a bad reproduction of one of the famous Gaudier drawings of him:

> Why does Nude Erect [New Directions] represent me with a wart on my nose which ain't in the original Gaudier??
> DETAIL, son DETAIL

There were frequent delays in getting his books out. For months each winter I was off skiing somewhere. Once he wrote:

> Are you doing anything? Of course, if you spend three-quarters of your time sliding down ice-cream cones on a tin tea-tray, if you can't be bothered with detail, why the hell don't you get Stan Nott over from London, who could run it. Then you can scratch yr arse on Pike's peak to yr 'eart's content.

And another time:

> Youse guys seem to think Ez is made of brass, with steel springs and no attrition. God damn delays for years and years beginning to get the old man down.

Once, when something had irritated him, he enclosed a little poem for me:

> Here lies our noble lord the Jaz
> Whose word no man relies on
> He never breathed an unkind word
> His promises are pizen.

That, of course, is a parody of John Wilmot, the Earl of Rochester's impromptu on Charles II:

> Here lies a great and mighty king,
> Whose promise none relies on;
> He never said a foolish thing,
> Nor ever did a wise one.

Pound never cared much for most of the books I published — except those of his friends. This was his comment once on the book selection at New Directions:

> ... possibly a politic move on Jaz's part, great deal of sewage to float a few boats. Possibly useful; nasty way to educate the public, four percent food, ninety-six percent poison.

Another time he wrote:

> Most of it is considerably better than the trype you print in yr. Lewd Directions Annual Crap-can ... As to Jaz's damlitantism/ why the hell don't he recognize LIVE mind as distinct from dead and stop dabbling. If he wants to READ books, let him ask WHAT. That might save him loading his pub/list with rubbish.

Pound once told the playwright Ronald Duncan: "Jaz has a very long spine and he is always breaking it skiing. So when I kick his butt about what he should publish, the message does not ascend to his brain."

Here is a passage from a letter that mystified me at first. Pound wrote, "Jaz., can't remember everything during your flits. Have you remembered to send Mrs. Dutch Holland (Regina) the Confucian stone classics for to show her you can do something else except split your britches? You gotta educate them at the top." This is the explication: I had been skiing at St. Anton in Austria. The Queen of Holland was there, a most amiable and democratic lady. She had invited me to join her party on a high-mountain ski tour. On the trip I fell down and split my pants. Now bless me if Queen Juliana didn't have a needle and thread in her little sitzpack. With motherly concern, Her Majesty sewed up my pants so I could get down the mountain without disgrace. I wrote this tale to Ezra as something to divert him. His reaction shows how his mind worked. He immediately said to himself, now I've got a contact with the Big People in Holland. A chance to convert Holland to Confucianism if I can get my translation of the *Ta Hio* to her. I sent the book, received a polite thank-you note from a secretary, but have noted no change in the Dutch national ethos.

One of Pound's dearest and most loyal friends was T. S. Eliot. Ezra helped get Eliot published and later edited the draft of *The Waste Land*. Their letters to each other—Eliot was "Old Possum" and Pound was "Br'er Rabbit"—are masterpieces of affectionate teasing. In this tone Pound wrote to me, "Eliot's low saurian vitality. When the rock was broken out hopped Marse Toad, alive and chipper, after three thousand or whatever years inclaustration. When Joyce and Wyndham L. have long since gaga'd or exploded, Old Possum will be totin' round de golf links and givin' bright nickels to the lads of 1987."

The inserts in Pound's business letters were always a delight. Here is a poem he sent me about Eliot entitled "The Right Reverend, Bidding Him Corajo," which means courage.

> Come now, old vulchuh
> Rise up from thy nest
> Stretch forth thy wing
> on Chimborazo's height
> Strip off thy BVDs and undervest
> Display thy whangus in its antient might
> The old scabs is a droppin' orf the world its sore
> and Men would smell thy corn-cob poipe once more.

Here is a nugget on Yeats, who had visited Rapallo: "The aged Yeats left yester. I had several serious reflections re doing a formal document requesting you to chloriform me before I get to that state. However, must be a trial to be Oirrish in Oireland."

As Pound aged, from about 1939, there was a gradual slippage. He never lost his wits, but, as he became more obsessed with economics and saving the world through monetary reform, his letters became more brief and elliptical. When we were putting out a new edition of *Guide to Kulchur*, I asked for some description for the jacket copy. All he answered was:

> Guide to Kulchur; a mousing round for a word or a shape, for an order, for a meaning and last of all for a philosophy. The turn came with Bunting's lines, "man is not an end-product, maggot asserts." The struggle was and still might be to preserve some of the values that make life worth living. And they are still mousing around for a significance in the chaos.

That says what he wanted to say, but without his old spirit.

1939 *Trip to U.S.*

A turning point in Pound's life was his trip back to the United States in 1939. He hadn't been in the States since 1910, and it proved to be a depressing experience. He had come over hoping to meet Roosevelt and certain members of Congress. He would tell them what to do about the national economy and international policy. But no one of importance in Washington would see him. This failure to be recognized as a thinker, not just as a poet, broke his spirit. Undoubtedly he appeared an eccentric screwball to those who did see him in Washington. One of his proposals was that, to avert war with Japan, the United States should trade Wake Island to the Japanese for a complete canon of the classic Noh plays. Such an idea demonstrates, I think, what the psychiatrists later diagnosed as *confabulation*, an inability to distinguish between fantasy and reality. Not being seen by Roosevelt led Pound to a paranoid hatred of him as we hear in the Rome broadcasts.

Some think that Pound's staying on in Italy when war broke out proves him a traitor. Not so. Many passages in his work, especially the Jefferson and Adams sections of the *Cantos*, show that he remained profoundly American during his expatriation. A major theme of the broadcasts is his concern for preserving the Constitution and the principles of the founding fathers, at least as he interpreted them. Pound stated that he wanted to come home, but he couldn't leave his old father, Homer, who was in an enfeebled state in the Rapallo hospital with a broken hip.

As for Pound's fascism, it is usually explained that he hoped that Mussolini would be strong enough to crack down on the Italian banks and believed that the fascist corporations, with which Il Duce had replaced labor unions, would fit into a Social Credit system. One of my theories about his fascism—and I have my own gift for confabulation—is that Pound identified Mussolini with one of his great heroes of the Renaissance, Sigismondo Malatesta of Rimini, to whom Cantos 8–11 are devoted. Sigismondo was not only a great warrior but a patron of artists and humanistic learning. Is it not possible that Pound imagined that he could persuade Mussolini to grant state patronage to writers and artists? Unfortunately, the only *borsa* that Mussolini gave was to Pirandello, who was a fascist.

Pound spent twelve years in St. Elizabeths after the federal court found him to be of unsound mind. I had been out of touch with him during the war years; mail did not go through to Italy and it was impossible to send him his royalties, so that, with Dorothy and Olga, he was living in penury in Olga's small villa in San Ambrogio above Rapallo. Their only income was what Olga earned giving English lessons. When I saw him in Washington I was troubled to see how he had aged after his experience in the Army's Disciplinary Training Center at Pisa. His confinement in a cage had brought on a nervous breakdown. Then he was moved to a tent and allowed to use a typewriter in the medical office. But most of *The Pisan Cantos* were drafted in handwriting in schoolchildren's notebooks given him by the Jewish chaplain. These are now at the Beinecke Library at Yale.

Sanity Question

In Dr. E. Fuller Torrey's notorious book, *The Roots of Treason: Ezra Pound and the Secret of St. Elizabeths*, the author, a student of the insanity defense and an authority on schizophrenia, attempts to prove that Pound was mentally sound and that a group of writers, which included T. S. Eliot, Archibald MacLeish, and myself, conspired with Dr. Overholser to protect Pound from trial. This is simply not true. As I told Torrey when he first interviewed me, I did not know Overholser until months after the sanity hearing. Torrey is now on the staff of St. Elizabeths but he came there after Ezra had departed and never knew him. Under the Freedom of Information Act, he obtained access to Pound's medical records and used them in such a way as to present his case.

Torrey says that Pound was well enough to stand trial, but I disagree. I saw Ezra several times soon after he reached Washington. No question about it, his head was in trouble. He could not concentrate, he could not arrange his thoughts in any kind of rational order, and he was confabulating. I had asked my lawyer, Julien Cornell, to see him and to report on his condition. After their meeting, Cornell called me to say: "Jaz, this won't wash. The man is not in his senses and couldn't possibly help me defend him." Cornell went on to say that when he had asked Ezra if he could get him anything, Ezra replied, "Well, I'd like to have a Georgian grammar. I want to write to Stalin about Confucius."

For a time, before he was moved to St. Elizabeths, Pound was held in Gallinger Hospital, a real snake pit full of maniacs and dangerous criminals. I visited him there and found him in terror, afraid for his life. "Jaz," he said, "I don't know what I'm doing here. I thought they were bringing me to Washington to send me on to Tokyo to help MacArthur convert the Japs from Shintoism to Confucianism."

I attended the sanity hearing, the necessary preliminary in his case to a trial, which was held before Judge Bolitha Laws, a courtly Southerner, in federal court. Three psychiatrists appeared for the government—Dr. Overholser of St Elizabeths, Dr. King of the Public Health Service, and Dr. Gilbert of Gallinger—and one, Dr. Wendell Muncie of Johns Hopkins, for the defense. All of them had had the opportunity to study Pound, some over a period of weeks. They were grilled for several hours by two lawyers from the Justice Department. Their terminology varied, but all four agreed that Pound was in no shape to stand trial. Cornell, Pound's London lawyer Arthur V. Moore, and most of Pound's friends agreed that temporary incompetency was the best defense. For my part, I had it much in mind that my cousin-by-marriage, Douglas Chandler, who had broadcast from Germany, had been given a long sentence.

The sanity hearing was a memorable experience for me. It made me proud to be an American. In some other countries Ezra would have been railroaded into prison, or worse. Ezra was not questioned and spoke only once when one of the government attorneys accused him of being a fascist. He was sitting at a small table below the bench with his head in his hands, but at these words he reared up out of his chair and shouted, "God damn it, I never was a fascist!" The jury took only a few minutes to decide that he was of unsound mind, and Judge Laws remanded him to St. Elizabeths to remain there until he was well enough to stand trial—which never happened.

In sum, the diagnosis of the four psychiatrists was "a paranoid state, with confabulation." Dr. Jerome Kavka, a Freudian on the St. Elizabeths staff who worked with Pound, diagnosed "severe narcissism," which means, I'm told, "excessive arrogance." No drugs or therapy were used, and he was given excellent care at St. Elizabeths. Gradually his power of concentration returned and he began writing. He wrote further *Cantos* and did his extraordinary versions of the *Confucian Odes* and of Sophocles' *Women of Trachis* and the *Elektra*, the latter in collaboration with his friend Rudd Fleming, a professor at the University of Maryland. With the help of a disciple, Marcella Spann, he put together his choice of poetry in the *Confucius to Cummings* anthology. He carried on an enormous correspondence, though by now his letters had become very elliptical and scrappy, with many unexplained references. For years he had always seemed to assume that his correspondents had read every book he had.

In St. Elizabeths

When he first came to St. Elizabeths, Pound was quartered in Howard Hall, a gloomy old building. Later Dr. Overholser moved him to Chestnut Ward, the senile ward, which was more cheerful. There he had his own cubicle with his books in orange crates and a table for his typewriter. There was an alcove by the window in the long hall with fairly comfortable chairs where he could receive his visitors. He was allowed to see anyone who was not a journalist. Many of the leading poets came to sit with him, as did I, from time to time. I was astonished at his good spirits, considering that many of the Chestnut Ward inmates were zombies who sat motionless on benches along the wall. Ezra was soon the king of the ward. A snap of his fingers would bring one of the mobile zombies to run his errands or to fetch an extra chair for his guests. Dorothy Pound had taken a small apartment near the hospital. She had lunch every day in the cafeteria, then came to sit with him, often helping him with his correspondence. Many of the letters to me of that period are in her hand.

After a few years in St. Elizabeths, Pound was almost himself again. His stories were as comical and various as ever. His remarkable memory was no longer impaired. Yet some confabulation persisted. One day he asked me to stay for lunch with him in the cafeteria. Our plates were brought to us by one of the zombies. Then another one came to the table and systematically tasted Pound's food. "What's this about?" I asked. "Don't you know," he said, not joking, "that Bernie Baruch is trying to have me poisoned?"[3] So sad. Then he went on, "I don't know why the Jews are after me. I sent them plans for rebuilding their temple in Jerusalem."

After some years Julien Cornell thought that he might be able to get Pound released on a writ of habeas corpus. He had been unable to find any precedent for holding a man in Pound's situation indefinitely if he were not a menace to society, as Pound certainly was not. Cornell drew up the papers, but Ezra would not let Dorothy, who was his legal guardian, sign them. "I'm going to come out of here," he told me, "only with flying colors and a personal apology from the President."

All during the years in St. Elizabeths, Pound kept up his "network" by correspondence. The network was made up of people all over the world who were committed to his literary and economic principles and who were prepared to do propaganda for them. He either controlled or influenced five tiny magazines: *Strike, Current, Four Pages,* Noel Stock's *Edge* in Australia, and William Cookson's *Agenda* in London. He also instigated the Square Dollar series of paperback books. But his name is seldom to be found in any of these publications, though it is easy to detect his contributions from the style. In those years he would sign nothing, not even a book contract, because he felt that his individuality had been stripped from him.

Dr. Overholser gave him grounds privileges in summer or when the weather was fine. He would carry his bathchair out onto the lawn, there to be surrounded by visitors and disciples. It was the Ezuversity all over again, his little academy. He would lean far back in the bathchair, the position we see in the Wyndham Lewis portrait that is now in the Tate in London. He loved to tease the squirrels. He would tie a peanut to a thread and toss it out to them. When the squirrel took it, he would jerk it away.

Among the most faithful of the disciples was the beautiful artist La Martinelli. She was perhaps twenty-five, with splendid red hair, and dressed in Victorian silk gowns—a figure out of a Pre-Raphaelite painting. She would sit at Ezra's feet with her sketch pad, drawing him very carefully. "Maestro," she would say, "please move your head a little to the left . . . a little more to the right." Her drawings were not very good, in fact, quite bad, but Ezra was much taken with her. To advance her career he persuaded his Milanese publisher, Vanni Scheiwiller, to bring out a small book of her work. In his text he described her as the finest draftsman since Botticelli. Another confabulation: *concitatio senectutis* (the arousing of desire in old men).

The disciples who came to the Ezuversity at St. Elizabeths were a mixed group. The worst of the lot was the notorious John Kasper, an extreme racist, who preached against "racial integration" in the South and ended up in jail in Tennessee. But there were many good ones: Hugh Kenner, who wrote the most important critical book about Pound, *The Pound Era*; Guy Davenport, now a professor at the University of Kentucky and perhaps the most brilliant avant-garde writer of his generation; David Gordon, who took up Chinese at Pound's suggestion and now teaches at the University of Maine; Marcella Spann Booth, now a professor of English at the University of Connecticut; and Dallam Simpson, who was the first to publish a book by Basil Bunting in this country.

In 1958 Pound was finally released from St. Elizabeths. There had been growing protest at his indefinite confinement from all over the world. It was an embarrassment to our State Department, as Christian Herter reported.[4] Dag Hammarskjöld of the

Pound at Spoletto around 1965.

United Nations gave his support. Eliot, MacLeish, Hemingway, Frost, and other eminent writers applied pressure in Washington. The actual mechanics of the release were accomplished by Gabriel Hauge, an economic adviser to President Eisenhower, who persuaded Sherman Adams, Eisenhower's chief of staff, to request the Justice Department to quash the old indictment for treason. Pound was at last a free man, permitted to return to Italy.

Old Age

Pound's old age was a sad one. Physical ailments added to his other problems. There were a few good years at his daughter Mary's castle above Merano in the Italian Alps, and visits with John Drummond and an Italian friend, Ugo Dadone, in Rome.[5] Then his condition deteriorated with severe prostatism and, far more crippling, an intense depression that no drug could relieve. I reported this to Dr. Overholser, who explained that clinical depression was often the sequel to paranoia when physical vitality became diminished. When I visited Pound in the early 1960s, he told me that he could no longer write at all because he couldn't get the fog out of his head. There were few more *Cantos*, though he did gather together a small volume of *Drafts & Fragments*, which New Directions published in 1968. These final cantos are of great beauty but they are very short and often fragmentary. He did not have the strength to write the grand paradisiacal closure that he had intended, in counterpart to Dante's *Paradiso*, though with Pound it was to have been the *paradiso terrestre*, the earthly paradise, which he hoped his economic reforms would usher in. The last line, where he left off, is "To be men not destroyers," preceded by a loving tribute to Olga Rudge which includes the tragic lines:

> That I lost my center
> > fighting the world
> The dreams clash
> > and are shattered.

Olga Rudge and Pound at Olga's house in San Ambrogio, 1963.

It was Olga Rudge who took care of him in his last years because Dorothy's health was also failing. Olga sheltered him in her little house in the San Trovaso district of Venice, where Pound had first come in 1908, and in her farmhouse at San Ambrogio on the mountainside above Rapallo. I visited them several times and can attest that the care Olga gave Ezra was both angelic and practical. She kept him going when he would otherwise have slipped away. There was, of course, no money for a nurse or servant, and it was a night and day job. She occupied his mind by coaxing him into recording the *Cantos*. He believed then that his work was no good and could not understand why students and admirers came to call on him.

Perhaps it was in the early 1960s that the much reported "silence" set in. Pound ceased to talk. He would go for hours without saying a word. I noticed that he followed conversations with his eyes, but he said nothing. About 1962, he told me that he did not talk because no one would listen to his economic ideas, and he quoted to me the legend that comes from the Book of Ecclesiastes and is repeated on one of the chapel scrolls in his favorite building in all Italy, the Tempio Malatestiana in Rimini, "tempus loquendi, tempus tacendi." (There is a time for speaking and there is a time to be silent.) His family has always interpreted the silence as a form of meditation, of monastic withdrawal, but this does not accord with his views on religion. He believed in such cults as the Eleusinian Mysteries,[6] not in Christianity or Buddhism. The appeal to him of Confucianism was precisely that it was ethics, not religion as most of us conceive it. Remembering what a great raconteur he had been in his prime, it was shattering for me to be with him in this perpetual muteness. I would talk my head off trying to divert him, to bring him some comfort in his desolation... but almost never got the slightest response.

Yet I do remember a few occasions when he spoke. One day in Venice, Olga wanted to go shopping and I took him to lunch at Montini's, a quiet trattoria that he had always liked. Not a word from him all during the meal. But when I happened to ask him, "Ezra, what was Djuna Barnes like when you knew her in

Olga Rudge and Pound in a gondola in Venice, 1962.

Paris?'' he suddenly answered: ''Waaal, she wasn't very cuddly.''
That old wit was there. And as I was saying goodbye, about to
leave Venice, and he knew I was going to London, where I
would see Eliot, he spoke again: ''Tell the Possum that the head-
ache pills came from a place behind the Chambre de Députés.''
Something remembered from fifty years in the past.

In 1967, Olga brought him to Paris for the publication of
French translations of some of his books. One Sunday I hired a
car and drove them out to see the chateau of Vaux-le-Vicomte.
Swinging his cane, Ezra walked briskly through the house and
the gardens. No comment whatever. But that evening he ut-
tered. He had been seeing his old friend Sam Beckett, who had
taken him to a performance of *Fin de Partie* (*Endgame*), the play in
which two characters are in garbage cans. Out of the blue he
said, ''C'était moi dans la poubelle.'' (I was the one in the garbage can.)

Last Visit to the U.S.

In that same year, Pound, accompanied by Olga, made his last visit to the United States. He attended a reception given by the Academy of American Poets at the New York Public Library. He was seated in a doganal chair at the end of the large room. As people came to speak to him, he would rise for each one, shake hands, but say nothing. However, when Marianne Moore, with whom he had corresponded since the days of *The Dial*, came to greet him, Marie Bullock took them off to a side room and stood guard at the door. But she let me peek in; Ezra was talking to Miss Moore with animation.

It made me so happy to see Ezra talking again. But the next week I was quite shattered when he said something that revealed the depth of his despair. In 1939 Pound's alma mater, Hamilton College, had given him an honorary doctorate of letters. At the 1967 commencement Hamilton was giving me a degree, largely, I think, because I was his publisher. Ezra and Olga came up to Clinton, New York, for the occasion. And it was a fine one. He marched in the academic procession and received a tremendous ovation when he entered the hall. He was courtly in acknowledging greetings but totally silent. That evening, as we were driving back to my home in Connecticut, we stopped at a Howard Johnson restaurant for some supper. One of Olga's problems in the later years was to get Ezra to eat. He had become very thin and, with his white beard and hair, looked like a beautiful old prophet. But my wife coaxed him into having apple pie with ice cream. As we left the restaurant and were going to the parking lot, I noticed that Ezra was missing. I checked the men's room; not there. Then I noticed a figure in the darkness moving slowly down toward the woods back of the building. "Ezra," I asked, when I got to him, "where are you going? The car is over there." Then came the saddest words I have ever heard. "Why don't you *discard* me here? Then I won't be any more trouble to anyone." All I could do was put my arms around him and tell him that we all loved him.

Pound with Walter Pilkington, the Librarian of Hamilton College, in 1967 when Laughlin got an honorary degree.

Pound died on November 1, 1972, at the age of 87. He is buried in San Michele, the island cemetery in the lagoon at Venice. His grave is in the part reserved for foreigners—exiled White Russian generals, Stravinsky, Sergei Diaghilev. There is no monument, just a simple stone plaque in the ground with ivy growing around it. Many urge that he should be moved home to this country, perhaps to Hailey, Idaho, where he was born. But Hailey is the end of nowhere. Let him rest where he is. He loved Venice, was often happy there, and some of the finest lines in the *Cantos* are about Venice.

I sat on the Dogana's steps
For the gondolas cost too much, that year,
And there were not 'those girls,' there was one face...
And the lit cross-beams that year in the Morosini...
  Gods float in the azure air.
Bright gods and Tuscan, back before dew was shed.
Light: and the first light before ever dew was fallen.

I conclude with some lines from a poem of my own, written to honor Ezra Pound:

Lie quiet, Ezra, there in your campo santo on San Michele
In paradisum te deducant angeli
To your city of Dioce, to Wagadu,
To your paradiso terrestre
What I have reft from you
I stole for love of you
Beloved, my master and my friend.

Pound and Laughlin, Rapallo, 1963.

POUND'S PEDAGOGY

I've always been grateful to the little fallen blossom on that stormy night in Crawfordsville, Indiana, who got Ezra canned from his only academic job at Wabash College. He had met a young lady abandoned by a theatrical company and given her innocent shelter—she slept in his bed, Ezra in the arm chair. The landlady squealed to the president of the college and he was invited to leave. Even if he had made fast time on the tenure track and replaced Billy Phelps at Yale, the *Cantos* would probably not have been written. They could not have been written in America. Pound had to sit on the steps of the Dogana and hear "a great Peeeeacock in the proide ov his oye" and see the gulls on the Serpentine and walk three roads below Rochecoart, "thinking of old days," to make the *Cantos*. It is a European poem by an American.

Pound was born a teacher, even if not destined to be a professor. He could not keep himself from teaching. In one way or another he was always teaching. The *Cantos* themselves are a kind of teaching. *Ut doceat, ut moveat, ut delectet.* They move us, they delight us, but above all they teach us. As Richard Sieburth says, "The Cantos are not fiction, but a dispensation of likenesses, a disposition of facts given by history, an arrangement of verities that inhere in Nature and Tradition. . . . Pound's job was simply to distribute or to circulate what had been placed in his care." "Distribute" and "circulate"—Sieburth's analogy here is with Pound's theories of money. But I think he has given us the perfect description of what a great teacher does. A great teacher presents verities and compares them so that students can judge for themselves.

Pound never received his Ph.D. from Penn, but he deserved it. His pedagogy took many forms. Like Odysseus he was *polumetis*, a man of many skills.

Prose Books

Pound's pedagogy has reached an audience much larger than the fortunate few who passed through Rapallo during the years of the Ezuversity, and here one thinks first, of course, of the prose books. I won't go into them at any length because it would take an entire book. But I will attempt a few thumbnail sketches.

First was *The Spirit of Romance*, published in 1910. This is an easygoing but very discerning account of the early Romance-language literatures. The troubadours, the *Chanson de Roland*, the *Poema del Mio Cid*, the Italian poets of the *dolce stil nuovo*, Dante, Villon, Lope de Vega, Camoens, and Renaissance Latin poets. *The Spirit of Romance* was based on what Pound learned from Professor Shepard at Hamilton and Professor Rennert at Penn—and on his research for lectures he gave at the Regent Street Polytechnic in London in 1909–1910. It was at one of these lectures that a beautiful young lady named Dorothy Shakespear first saw him, but it took her five years to persuade her parents that she might marry the handsome but indigent poet. *The Spirit of Romance* is judgmental. Even as an adolescent Ezra knew what was bad and what was good in literature. William Carlos Williams, his classmate at Penn, describes him as "arrogant." But he proved his assessments with fine translations.

In London, Pound was exposed to the world of contemporary art. (He had, of course, seen old masters in Venice and Florence.) Perhaps his greatest enthusiasm was for the young French sculptor Henri Gaudier-Brzeska, whom Pound promoted vigorously and generously—as he did many writers: Frost, Eliot, Joyce, H. D., Wyndham Lewis, Zukofsky, and others. Lewis christened Pound the "Pantechnicon" for his entrepreneurial energy. Gaudier's "hierarchical" head of Pound, abstract and massive—now on loan to the Tate Gallery in London—is one of the masterpieces of modern sculpture. (It has an interesting feature; the back of the head resembles a scrotum.)

Gaudier enlisted in the French Army and was killed in 1915. The letters that he wrote to Pound from the trenches are most moving. Pound's second prose book, published in 1916, was *Gaudier-Brzeska: A Memoir.* This is the beginning of his teaching about art. He analyzes Gaudier's work and the Vorticist movement.

There were other early prose books, such as *Pavannes and Divisions* (1918) and *Instigations* (1920). In 1954 T. S. Eliot gathered the best from these earlier books, combining them with parts of *Make It New* (1934) and *Polite Essays* (1937) to produce the enlarged volume of *Literary Essays*. All of these essays teach in one way or another. The book has sections on "The Art of Poetry," "The Tradition," and "Contemporaries." "Notes on Elizabethan Classicists" and "Translations of Greek" contain anthologies. The remarkable essay on Henry James is taxonomic. Because Eliot edited the texts, the tone and style are well behaved.

In 1934, with the *ABC of Reading,* which is a sequel to *How To Read,* there is a change in the method of Pound's propaedeutic prose. Not entirely abrupt, perhaps, because it follows from Pound's epistolary style. The paragraphs became shorter and the sentences expostulatory. Many of them are memorable apothegms—apodictic and colorful. Pound's beloved "gists and piths" came into play. The statements punch hard and make me remember the story in *A Moveable Feast* of Hemingway giving Pound boxing lessons in Paris, teaching him to jab with his left. We are moving toward the "rock drill, drilling it into their heads." The *ABC* is the most widely studied of Pound's prose books in American colleges. I need hardly brief it, except to say that Pound again uses his anthological method to show the poetry that makes up his "canon."

With *Guide to Kulchur* in 1938, which Pound always called "*Kulch,*" the hard-hitting tone of *ABC of Reading* is applied to more complex materials—the whole range of Pound's cultural interests. The preface to *Kulch* reads:

> This book is not written for the over-fed. It is written for men who have not been able to afford an university education or for young men, whether or not threatened with universities, who want to know more at the age of fifty than I know today, and whom I might conceivably aid to that object.
>
> I am fully aware of the dangers inherent in attempting such utility to them.

I suppose that *Kulch* is an arrogant book, but I find it the richest of Pound's prose texts, certainly the one that stirs up the most argument from my students at Brown. It ranges through history, art, literature, philosophy, Confucianism, economics, government, the concept of the Vortex, music, and anthropology. Let me give you one short sample of the method and wisdom of *Kulch*:

> Knowledge is NOT culture. The domain of culture begins when one HAS "forgotten-what-book."

That may sound like a joke, but it isn't.

We see Pound teaching musical theory in *Antheil and the Treatise on Harmony*, published in 1924, and now available in F. Murray Schafer's *Ezra Pound and Music*. George Antheil was a young avant-garde composer who came to Paris in 1923. Like the Dadaists, Antheil was a showman.[1] He would put a revolver on the piano when he played. His notorious composition was the *Ballet Mécanique*, scored for nine pianos, xylophones, loudspeakers, whistles, and an airplane propeller in the orchestra. Pound liked Antheil's work, promoted him, and asked him to orchestrate his opera *Le Testament*, the libretto being poems of Villon. Most of the book is devoted to Antheil with Pound's curious treatise on harmony appended. "Harmony" seems an odd term for Pound to have used. His interest was in the melodic line as related to the sound length, the weight of the words in his text. I know nothing about music so the *Treatise* baffles me. Most of the discussion of harmony appears to come from talks with Antheil, who later said he had been misunderstood. Pound's major theories are the Great Bass and Absolute Rhythm as the breath pattern of the whole composition. The Great Bass is not like an organ bass, or the drone of an Indian tambura, but a "basis," Schafer explains, "like the keel line of a ship, exercising centripetal pull over everything above it." Pound elaborates in *Guide to Kulchur*, "The 60, 72 or 84, or 120 per minute is a BASS or basis. It is the bottom note of the harmony." Schafer points out that Absolute Rhythm was "a superior rhythm which was part of the poetic idea itself, not a discipline over which the poem was strung." For Pound music was song, the *motz el son* of the troubadours. To understand Pound's ideas it is easier to read Schafer's *Ezra Pound and Music* than to tackle *Antheil and the Treatise on Harmony*.

Pound's writings against the banking system are pedagogical, political, and violently polemical. His theories are not easy to understand. Most people think of him as a Social Crediter, but Social Credit was only a part of the picture. He drew not only on C. H. Douglas, but on Silvio Gesell's notion of stamp scrip, St. Ambrose's attacks on usury, the history of the Monte dei Paschi bank in Siena, the ideas of Mencius and Confucius on taxation, the researches into coinage of Alexander Del Mar, the Fascist corporations, cullings from Adams, Jefferson, and Van Buren, and from the books of some fifteen contemporary anti-bank economists. To untangle these sources, Pound's *ABC of Economics* is not the best text because he wrote it as a simplistic primer. It is better to study the separate more specialized economic pieces in the *Selected Prose* or in *Impact*.

Anthologies

Another aspect of Pound's teaching was the editing of anthologies. These collections enabled him to publicize contemporary poets he liked and to establish critical values. His anthologies were *Des Imagistes* (1914), which launched H.D. and the Imagist movement; *Catholic Anthology* (1915), which included Yeats, Eliot, and Williams; *Profile* (1932) with "poems which have stuck in my memory and which may possibly define their epoch"; *Active Anthology* (1933), the poets Pound thought were "developing"; and *Confucius to Cummings* (1964), which Pound called "*Kung to Cgs*" — this last a joint project with Marcella Spann, a St. Elizabeths disciple, with Pound's comments on some of the poets.

Indiscretions, a fifty-page *rigolade* of family history and autobiography, was part of a series of books, which Pound selected for his Paris friend William Bird of the Three Mountains Press.[2] Pound called the series "The Inquest" — "authors who have set out from five very different points to tell the truth about *moeurs contemporaines*, without fake, melodrama, conventional ending." The six authors were Pound, Ford Madox Ford (*Women and Men*), Hemingway (*In Our Time*), William Carlos Williams (*The Great American Novel*), B. C. Windeler (*Elimus*), and B. M. G. Adams, a pseudonym of Pound's girlfriend, Bride Scratton (*England*). They all came out in 1923, except Hemingway's, which was published in 1924.

Reviews

Literary reviews were important for Pound in several ways. First financially; he was impoverished during the London years. His books brought in little and Dorothy had only a small allowance. Pound lived by doing reviews and articles, chiefly for the *New Age*. The pieces are richly pedagogical: "I Gather the Limbs of Osiris," "The Approach to Paris," "Patria Mia." When the *New Age* lost its music critic, Ezra grabbed the job, though he had no training for it. He wrote, as I have previously mentioned, under the name of "William Atheling." (These pieces will be found in Schafer's *Ezra Pound and Music*.) Later he became an art critic as "B. H. Dias" — these pieces to be found in Harriet Zinnes's *Ezra Pound and Art*. Many of Pound's prose writings for *Poetry* and later for *The Little Review* and for *The Dial* are pedagogy.

Pound in front of painting by Dorothy Pound, 1939.

Editorial Control

Pound usually tried to gain control of the editorial policy of the reviews for which he acted as advisor or foreign editor. His letters to Harriet Monroe, telling her whom to print are merciless. But Harriet's letters to Ezra show she was not intimidated; she gave him back as good as she got. In the end Pound gave up trying to "eggerkate" Harriet. He moved on to Margaret Anderson at *The Little Review*. Here the pattern of the correspondence is about the same, though Margaret printed more of what Ezra recommended than did Harriet.

One of Pound's most responsive epistolary students was the New York lawyer John Quinn. Pound persuaded Quinn to buy works by Gaudier, Lewis, and Epstein; to subsidize his scouting work for *The Little Review*; to arrange his connection with *The Dial*; and to help Joyce in many ways.

Pound also influenced the policies of Samuel Putnam's *New Review*, Lincoln Kirstein's *Hound & Horn*, *The Smart Set* (not much), Mencken's *American Mercury* (not much), Harriet Weaver's *Egoist* (where he planted Joyce's *Portrait of the Artist*), Wyndham Lewis's *Blast*, and Charles Henri Ford's *Blues*. Eliot gave him pages in *The Criterion*, but less often when Pound's articles became extremely tendentious.

In the economic-political field Pound instructed the readers of *The New English Weekly*, Gorham Munson's *New Democracy* (until his anti-Semitism became too much for Munson), *The British Union Quarterly* (a Mosely organ), the *Rassegna Monetaria*, and the Rapallo paper *Il Mare*.

In 1927 Pound got his own review, *The Exile*, backed by Pascal Covici in Chicago, but it lasted for only four numbers. *The Exile* was in essence another of Pound's anthologies. It printed what he thought would instruct young writers.

There were several cases in which Pound achieved the extensive control of editorial policy that he sought. These were Noel Stock's *Edge* in Australia, Ronald Duncan's *Townsman* in London, and William Cookson's *Agenda*, also in London. (*Agenda* is still active as the voice and school of Pound in England, just as Terry Terrell's *Paideuma* is the voice of Pound studies in this country.)

From St. Elizabeths he inspired Henry Swabey's *Four Pages* (1950), David Gordon's *Academia Bulletin* (1956), William McNaughton's *Strike* (1956), and William E. French's *Current* (1955). Few of Pound's contributions to these leaflets are signed but they are identifiable from his style. I should also mention again the Square Dollar Series, dollar paperbacks which Pound's St. Elizabeths disciple, David Horton, published under his guidance.

Academy

Long before the Ezuversity, Pound dreamed of founding his own academy. It was to be a college of the arts. In a letter to Harriet Weaver in 1914 he set forth the curriculum: "That the arts, INCLUDING poetry and literature, should be taught by artists, by practicing artists, *not* by sterile professors." And "that the arts should be gathered together for the purpose of interenlightenment.... The art school, meaning 'paint school' needs literature for backbone, ditto the musical academy, etc." Pound was simply ahead of his time. This is the kind of program you will find in operation today at Cal Arts in Valencia and at the Arts College of U Cal Santa Barbara. (No doubt Pound hoped that Miss Weaver would endow his college of arts. She didn't; but she did, at Pound's urging, endow Joyce very liberally for his whole life.)

Network

Failing to get his arts college, Pound set about constructing an "academy by mail," which I like to call the "Network." In 1928 Pound wrote to James Vogel: "The utility of education or of knowing the subject is mainly to know *what* one *needn't* bother to do. *The pt. from which* one can start to do one's own bloody bizniz." And in the same letter he wrote: "It takes about 600 people to make a civilization. There were umpteen billions of unbreached barbarians in the North woods when Athens, etc." Pound set out to recruit his chosen six hundred by mail. Whenever he spotted a special intelligence in a book or magazine he would invite correspondence. And he encouraged one correspondent to recruit others. In his letters to me, he would urge me to "go see X, find out if there's anything in his bean," or "get Y in touch with Z." Sometimes the Network produced results. Pound pushed William Carlos Williams to read C. H. Douglas. On page 213 of *Paterson* Williams reproduced a credit reform tract and in 1936 he gave a talk at the University of Virginia on "The Attack on Credit from a Cultural Viewpoint."

(Pound's faith in the six hundred, his Light Brigade, made life easier for his publisher. He never fussed when a book had small sales. He assumed that a few copies would find receptive readers who would pass the word on to others.)

Manifestoes

Related to the Network were various manifestoes planted in magazines. The one in *Blast* was, I suspect, mostly written by Lewis, but Pound sent one of his own to Harriet Monroe in 1915, though I haven't tracked down whether she printed it. A typical manifesto is the one he sent to John Drummond, one of his most faithful disciples, in 1932 for the Cambridge magazine, *Contemporaries*[3]:

1. The critic most worth respect is the one who actually causes an improvement in the art he criticizes.
2. The best critic of next rank is the one who most focuses attention on the best work.
3. The pestilence masking itself as a critic distracts attention from the best work, either to secondary work that is more or less "good" or to tosh, to detrimental work, dead or living snobisms, or to indefinite essays on criticism.

Translations

The impulse for some of Pound's greatest translations was certainly didactic. The *Cantos* are the most interlingual of poems. I've counted bits of thirteen different languages in them. Pound told me that a poet could not do without at least three languages. If Pound translated something it was usually because it fitted into his canon, his total tradition, and because he believed that younger writers, and critics, could profit from having it in English.

Chinese was Pound's greatest literary interest—and greatest success. He began studying Confucius around 1915 when Allen Upward loaned him a translation of the *Chung Yung* and at about the same time the widow of the great Oriental scholar Ernest Fenollosa deposited with him her husband's notebooks. From these came the great poems of *Cathay* which, as Eliot said, "invented Chinese poetry for our time." (Arthur Waley came later.)[4] Pound never made finer poems than "The Bowmen of Shu" or "The River Merchant's Wife." Prior to *Cathay* the only translations much good as poetry were the French versions in Judith Gautier's *Livre du Jade*, on which Kenneth Rexroth later based the tone of his Chinese translations.

Pound loved slang. His conversations and his letters were laced with it. Did he think of slang as a teaching method or as a form of criticism? Its use became very interesting in the translations—or should we call them adaptations?—which he did of two Sophocles plays with his friend Professor Rudd Fleming in the St. Elizabeths days. First came the *Elektra* (with Fleming), then *The Women of Trachis*.

This exercise began, I suspect, as diversion. But it grew serious when Pound and his Greek coach got their teeth into the work. It gave Pound the opportunity to make certain critical statements about the Greek myths and the Greek ethos, statements that could be accentuated by putting parts of the speeches into slang.

In Pound's critical books Sophocles is barely mentioned. What turned him to the tragedies late in life? Guy Davenport credits Pound's new interest to his reading of F. R. Earp, whom Pound called "the only man who knew anything about Greek." Certainly Pound didn't think of himself in his years of incarceration as a "tragic" figure. On my visits to St. Elizabeths I always found him, after the first weeks of shock, amazingly cheerful. Perhaps a clue lies in the dedication to *The Women of Trachis*. It is dedicated to Pound's Japanese friend Katue Kitasono with the request that he show it to the Minoru, the actors of the Noh Theatre in Tokyo, "if they can be persuaded to add it to their repertoire." Pound had always wanted to write a Noh play, as far back as when Yeats wrote his. I believe he thought the *Trachiniae* was a good text for a Noh play. In a note he writes that the Noh "presents the highest peak of Greek sensibility" and is "nearest the original form of the God-Dance." But a Noh play full of slang? Noh speech is ceremonial.

In *Women of Trachis* the choruses are not in slang. For them

Pound wrote poetry, not attempting to reproduce the Greek meters but divising his own strophic form and a style-tone which is reminiscent of that in the *Homage to Sextus Propertius*. It was his interpretation of what Greek choral music and dancing may have been like.

KHOROS : KUPRIS bears trophies away.
Str.   Kronos' Son, Dis and Poseidon,
         There is no one
                  shaker unshaken.
         Into dust go they all.
         Neath Her they must
                give way.

Ant.   TWO gods fought for a girl,
         Battle and dust!
         Might of a River with horns
                  crashing.
         Four bulls together
                  Shall no man tether,
         Akheloös neither,
                  lashing through Oneudai

Most of the speeches are done colloquially with slang to give them tang. Here is Herakles (in the mask of divine agony) as the poison of Nessus is burning him up:

Holy Kanea, where they build holy altars,
done yourself proud, you have,
nice return for a sacrifice:
    messing me up.
I could have done without these advantages
And the spectacle of madness in flower,
    incurable, oh yes.
Get someone to make a song for it,
Or some chiropractor to cure it.
A dirty pest,

> take God a'mighty to cure it and
> I'd be surprised to see Him
> coming this far ...

There is nothing literal in Pound's translation. He skips phrases that bore him. He compresses. Slang helps him to do it. When the nurse brings news of Deianira's death (Pound calls her "Daysair") and the chorus badgers her for details, Pound has the nurse reply tersely, "That's all. You heard me." A passage which Gilbert Murray translated as:

> Go then my son. To have done the right, though late
> The knowledge came, must needs be fortunate

Pound reduces to:

> Well, get going. A bit late, but a good job's worth a bonus

My favorite is what Pound does with the last words of Herakles, *chalubos lithokolleton stomion.* Murray has:

> set me a brake
> On stony lips, steel hard and true

and Pound:

> And put some cement in your face,
> Reinforced concrete ...

In performance, the slang sometimes brings laughs in serious moments, but on the whole it works, producing a lively play which holds the attention of the audience.

Professor Fleming tells me that the translation of the *Elektra* actually preceded that of *Women of Trachis,* but the *Elektra* was never submitted for publication. Evidently Pound did not think it good enough. I strongly disagree. Recently a reading was presented by the Classic Stage Company in New York which was very comical in Pound's slang yet powerful and in a strange way profoundly Greek in spirit. Pound and Fleming used the 1904 translation of Sir Richard C. Jebb as a guide, condensing the text heavily to eliminate old-fashioned rhetoric and get down to the terror of the mythic story. The original typescript is now in the Firestone Library at Princeton. The typing looks like Pound's but some of the glosses must be Fleming's.

The choruses are done colloquially. Technically most interesting is the long passage beginning *o philtaton mnemeion anthropon emoi* (line 1126). Here Pound has introduced the heading "ELEKTRA'S KEENING" with stage direction for antiphonal rendering, the chorus to echo in Greek the lines that Elektra speaks in English. For her lament, which is greatly condensed, Pound has devised a tone that I don't think I have seen elsewhere in his work and a metric that seems to echo Sappho's Adonic:

> All that is left me
> my hope was Orestes
> dust is returned me,
> dust that is all of him
> flower that went forth . . .

Troubadours

Pound spent some twenty years translating the Provençal poems of the troubadours, the eleventh- to twelfth-century poets of the *langue d'oc*: poets Arnaut Daniel, Bertran de Born, Ventadorn and others. He became convinced that they were an important link in his tradition of love poetry. He was intrigued by the intricacy of the Provençal verse forms. Approximately 2600 troubadour texts survive and in them Jacques Roubaud distinguishes 900 different stanzaic rhyme schemes. Fearless as always, Pound attempted to reproduce these patterns. His ingenuity was remarkable, but to get the rhymes he often had to use archaic words or invert natural word order.

Thus his versions are not as readable as those, say, of Paul Blackburn, who follows the stanzaic structure but does not struggle for rhymes.

Was Pound's long preoccupation with the troubadours time wasted? I don't think so because from that effort he learned so much about the weight and musical duration of vowel sounds. The musical phrasing of his operas based on texts of Villon and Cavalcanti shows the influence of the troubadours' *motz el son* — words with sound to make songs—and especially of Arnaut Daniel, the inventor of the sestina. Pound studied troubadour musical notation from manuscripts of Arnaut he found in the Ambrosiana in Milan and collaborated with Walter Morse Rummel and Agnes Bedford on modern scores.

Pound did a similar job of restoration for Dante's friend Guido Cavalcanti, the most intellectual of the poets of the *dolce stil nuovo*. "Thought cuts through thought with a clean edge," Pound said of him. Guido was Pound's exemplar of the best in medievalism. He kept revising his translations of Cavalcanti's greatest *canzone*, the "Donna mi Pregha." His final version became Canto 36:

> A Lady asks me
>   I speak in season
> She seeks reason for an affect, wild often
> That is so proud he hath Love for a name

In his translations Pound often tried to show what a poet is doing in a poem, and what makes it different from what had been done before. His versions of Rimbaud and Laforgue are good examples of this.

Parody

Parody was a part of Pound's pedagogical arsenal. This is what he did with a traditional song:

ANCIENT MUSIC

Winter is icummen in,
Lhude sing Goddamm,
Raineth drop and staineth slop,
And how the wind doth ramm!
      Sing: Goddamm.
Skiddeth bus and sloppeth us,
An ague hath my ham.
Freezeth river, turneth liver,
      Damn you, sing: Goddamm.
Goddamm, Goddamm, 'tis why I am, Goddamm,
      So 'gainst the winter's balm.
Sing goddamm, damm, sing Goddamm,
Sing goddamm, sing goddamm, DAMM.

NOTE. — *This is not folk music, but Dr. Ker writes that the tune is to be found under the Latin words of a very ancient canon.*

And with these epigrams in the tone of the Latin first-century poet Martial:

EPITAPH

Leucis, who intended a Grand Passion
Ends with a willingness-to-oblige.

PHYLLIDULA

Phyllidula is scrawny but amourous,
Thus have the gods awarded her,
That in pleasure she receives more than she can give;
If she does not count this blessed
Let her change her religion.

THE PATTERNS

Erinna is a model parent,
Her children have never discovered her adulteries.
Lalage is also a model parent,
Her offspring are fat and happy.

Mauberley involves some parody of Théophile Gautier and Laforgue. Parody is an element in the "anti-establishment" sections of the *Propertius*. Not so easy to detect is the use of parody in Pound's versions of the *Confucian Odes*. These were seldom literal translations. Sometimes Pound did them in his colloquial style. But often he would parody a model in traditional English verse to convey his sense of the original Chinese poem. An example of his intercultural and his synchronic concerns.

Letters

I have left to the last what may have been the most valuable of Pound's way of teaching. Let me call it the "tutorial" of his letters—instructions that reached hundreds of students, voluntary or involuntary. He wrote me over five hundred letters and only a few of them did not teach. I'm afraid that I seldom completed my reading assignments—the autobiography of Martin Van Buren or the complete works of Alexander Del Mar—but what a delight these letters were. They were written in the inimitable Ezratic lingo. The lively and humorous sentences jump off the page.

His letters to me were usually short, but for what he could do in full voice I urge you to read the 1916–17 series of letters to Iris Barry, a young American poet whose work caught his eye. In ten pages he tells her everything she need know—how to write, what to read—to launch her career. These are in the *Selected Letters* volume.

At a more technical level is a remarkable long letter of 1926 to Archibald MacLeish, now in the MacLeish archive of the Library of Congress. Archie had sent Ezra a new poem, "The Bleheris," and asked for criticism. He got it. "You understand I am putting on the heavy hammer," Pound wrote back, "If I don't, the criticism is no use, and we get off into mere conversation and politeness." He went through the poem line by line, pointing out the faults and suggesting improvements. This is typical of Pound's helpfulness to other writers.

A final letter reveals another and surprising variety of Pound's pedagogy—teaching carpentry. This document came to light only last year when Jill Janows, the producer of a documentary on William Carlos Williams, visited 9 Ridge Road in Rutherford. Looking for photographs, Williams's son found a shoebox full of old letters from writers. Among them was one from Pound giving Williams complete instructions for building himself a *patino*—a Rapallo pontoon-boat used for swimming. In it were detailed drawings for each part of the boat, measurements in centimeters for cutting each board, and advice about which screws to use. It must have made Pound happy to think of his old friend rowing down the Passaic River in a Rapallo patino.

WALKING AROUND
A WATER-BUTT

In the Water-Butt

BY EZRA POUND (1907)

There is a new young person on our street, a perfectly new young person. I am not sure that I entirely approve of the perfectly new young person. Sometimes I fear that she is efficient and I live in horror of people whose efficiencies are apparent.

No one whom I know knows the new young person, therefore I do not as yet know the aforementioned perfectly new young person. She smiled at me the other day but I am not sure that the smile was utterly comforting: she has not as yet instructed her small brother to scrape an acquaintance with me, altho I should be only too glad to present him with a sword bayonet or an old foil or some such trifle which would delight his heart and keep his mother occupied with worrying about the particular manner in which he would commit suicide next. I assure you that the sword bayonet is quite harmless, because I spoiled the edge of it chopping wood in my undergraduate days. However, this does not affect the perfectly new young person.

This morning contrary to my wont I was aroused at an ungodly early hour: looking out my boudoir window to see "wot t'ell" the matter was

I beheld the young person fussing with a horse. She rides straddle: oh no, not "as a man," despite the fact that I am an anachronism I will not commit that. She rides astride as, oh as the reformation people did on that iron horse in the Nuremberg Schloss . . . Where the old german lady will tell you all about divers varieties of spikings, pointing out the pincers and pot-hooks and varified instruments of nipping, and after describing certain processes whereby a human was dissected and bisected and multisected into sanguiniferous hash and then scorched to a frazzle, she will end with "Und dey killet heem, TEED".

The young person to my horror was not content with saddling her destrier. She rubbed him with heathen implements and poked his feet and smeared black stuff on his nails, pardon "hooves".

After these complications (I fear she is efficient after all) she bestrode the beast and disappeared around her house. A moment later she clattered down the concrete driveway and was gone.

I had not decided whether or no I liked her seat when I was again disturbed by the "clunk-tap" of a horse moving, I arose again in order that I might further observe her manner of sitting the nag. "For," thought I, "the young person has forgotten something, and no wonder considering that it is quite impossible that anyone should be fully awake at this hour of the day ("day" strictly by courtesy).

The sight which met me was not pleasing. It was another young person with clothes to match its horse. He also clanked up the drive and disappeared. As he did not reappear either on the porch or at the stables I conclude he hid himself somewhere in the shade of the kitchen.

He had been out of sight for at least forty seconds when I was distressed by more hoof-swatts from the other direction. "Heavens!" said I to the wall, with unusual restraint, "is our erstwhile quiet neighborhood to be turned into a corral or a horse-pond, simply because the new young person arises at midnight?"

It was however the young person herself and no newcomer. She sulked at the turn of the road (it is below a high wall and terrace and curves in a quarter-circle). For some four minutes I awaited developments. The young centaur evidently slept somewhere in the region of the back door, at least he remained invisible. She, the new young person, departed, but her expression was less in tune with the "morning" wind.

"Hmm," said I, "here is fine food for the worms of tragedy. I will garb myself and descend against her next returning and thereby out of the infinite kindness of my heart spare these two young innocents much grief and lamentation, much dole and bitter teen. There is already enough sunlight for me to read by and I will peruse the morning paper, or haply if it have not yet come (and it hadn't) I will ensconce my soul in Sordello, that it may seem as if my custom to arise with the dawn and fill my belly with the east wind and my mind with goodly instruction. This will also give me opportunity to become distantly acquainted with the new young person, who despite her apparent efficiency has very nice hair."

With such benevolence at heart I arrayed myself in what may by the tolerance be termed clothing and descended.

The thermometer had fallen thirty degrees in the night, I opened to that sublime line of Browning's

> And a cat's in the water-butt
> ("Mesmerism", *stanza* 2).

Thereafter I shivered in my tennis rags for half an hour, even untill the bearer of morning news was in sight at which time (the perfectly new young person having shown no signs of returning), I should have gone into the house had not the person with clothes to match his horse come out of the driveway.

I arose and whistled at him. "She came back while you were back of the house. You have missed her. She has gone."

"Wath she on horth-back? Which way did she go?" Now if this cub had possessed a spark of sense he would first have gone to the stables to see whether her horse was there, if there he would have prepared it for her riding and if gone he would have deduced that its mistress was aboard. Also the lisp irritated me (a lisp after a half hour's freezing on a July morning breeze is utterly inexcusable; if his teeth had chattered I could have sympathized).

As it was I made a severe full-arm gesture toward the Northwest, and remarked scornfully "No! when I beheld her she was mounted on the sacred white elephant of the Rhajmutami and attended by half the retinue of the Sahib Baltummerak."

He did not thank me, and I continued addressing the place where he had been. "And furthermore young man, if you would watch and wait in a sensible place instead of trying to sponge a breakfast from her cook, (who if she is up is certainly in no pleasant mood at this time of night) you would be less of a nuisance to Miss . . . ah to Miss . . . to ah your friend and myself."

As he was already out of sight it made very little difference what I said. They have not come back yet: either of them.

But I have relieved my feelings by writing to a teacher's agency explaining the relation of divers things in heaven and in earth; notably that I am not competing with the Chinese and that I decline to part with the fruits of my learning for less than the wage of a carpenter's apprentice. I do ye to wit moreover that I have no especial desire to instruct the budding idea in the art of shooting teutonic grammar or in tracing the interstices of the grecian verb, but it is written that man shall not live by verse alone.

I shall however sharpen that sword-bayonet before I present it to her younger brother.

(signed) GEOFRY STOWELL*

*   *   *

WATER-BUTT : A large open-headed cask set up on end to receive rainwater from a roof. (O.E.D.)

Pound always set his sights high. Nothing but the best. When I was studying with him at his Ezuversity in 1935 he advised me not to waste time trying to write stories. Stendhal, Flaubert, James, Ford, and Joyce, he told me, had done all that could be done with the novel. They had finished it off. *Ne plus ultra.* Reading with enjoyment, but not with admiration, his early story, "In the Water-Butt," which has slumbered for

* *[It has not been possible to identify "Geofry Stowell." Spelling and punctuation errors corrected. Orthography left intact. Ed.]*

seventy years in his files and now is in the Pound Archive at Yale's Beinecke Library, I see how right he was—at least in his own case. In an arch way the sketch has a certain charm, but it hardly advances the art of fiction. Yet it does give insight into what "Ra," as he was then called, was like when he was a graduate student in Romance languages at Penn. He comes through as exuberant, cocky—and sophomoric. Still, there are flashes of better things to come. There are foreshadowings of certain kinds of humor that would turn up in the comic poems in *Personae* or in his autobiographical *Indiscretions*. And there are tones in the story that point toward the lingo of his fabulously funny letters.

The typescript at the Beinecke is not dated, but Pound's bibliographer Donald Gallup deduces that "The Water-butt" was written in 1907. There is no mention of it in Pound's letters to his parents, to whom he usually reported what he was doing. This may confirm the year at Penn, when he was living at home in Wyncote, near Philadelphia. (Pound does speak later in the family letters of a novel that he destroyed.) There is nothing about "The Water-butt" in Noel Stock's 1970 biography nor in the extensive new research which Humphrey Carpenter and John Tytell have done for their forthcoming books on Pound. But in scanning Stock I came on a passage that could refer to it. Stock quotes from a letter Pound wrote to his friend L. Burton Hessler in 1907 in which he said, "... Am preparing a little booklet of satire that may amuse you slightly. It is a teeny weeny bit caustic in places but you won't mind, and the world is so very ridiculous that one can scarcely help smiling now and then." "Satire . . . ridiculous . . . smiling," that might be "The Water-butt."

Browning

The title of the piece is from Robert Browning, a line in his poem "Mesmerism," one of the "dramatic romances."

All I believed is true!
  I am able yet
  All I want, to get
By a method as strange as new:
Dare I trust the same to you?

If at night, when doors are shut,
  And the worm-wood picks,
  And the death-watch ticks
And the bar has a flag of smut,
And a cat's in the water-butt—

  *   *   *

If since eve drew in, I say,
  I have sat and brought
  (So to speak) my thought
To bear on the woman away,
Till I felt my hair turn grey—

And so on for twenty-seven rheumy-rhymey stanzas.

In 1909, when he was so beguiled by Browning, Pound responded with his own "Mesmerism," using the waterlogged cat for his epigraph:[1]

MESMERISM

"And a cat's in the water-butt."—ROBERT BROWNING

Aye you're a man that! ye old mesmerizer
Tyin' your meanin' in seventy swadelin's,
One must of needs be a hang'd early riser
To catch you at worm turning. Holy Odd's bodykins!

"Cat's i' the water butt!" Thought's in your verse-barrel,
Tell us this thing rather, then we'll believe you,

You, Master Bob Browning, spite your apparel
Jump to your sense and give praise as we'd lief do.

You wheeze as a head-cold long-tonsilled Calliope,
But God! what a sight you ha' got o' our in'ards,
Mad as a hatter but surely no Myope,
Broad as all ocean and leanin' man-kin'ards.

Heart that was big as the bowels of Vesuvius,
Words that were wing'd as her sparks in eruption,
Eagled and thundered as Jupiter Pluvius,
Sound in your wind past all signs o' corruption.

Here's to you, Old Hippety-Hop o' the accents,
True to the Truth's sake and crafty dissector,
You grabbed at the gold sure; had no need to pack cents
Into your versicles.
                              Clear sight's elector!

As George Bornstein has pointed out: "Couched in the form, language and meters of Browning, the poem identifies those characteristics of Browning's poetry which Pound admired and sought to adapt for his own verses." In 1983, when I was interviewing Pound's friend the poet Basil Bunting for Lawrence Pitkethly's documentary, Bunting remarked that Pound was about forty years behind in his poetic taste when he came to London in 1908. Browning, Rossetti, Arthur Symons, Ernest Dowson, and Bliss Carman were some of his early models. It was not until about 1912, when he had read Yeats, and Ford Madox Ford had ridiculed his archaic and stilted language, that he began to use an idiom that might be called modern. In "The Water-butt," Pound writes, "I will ensconce my soul in *Sordello*, that it may seem as if my custom to arise with the dawn and fill my belly with the east wind and my mind with goodly instruction." (An odd bit of syntax.)

As late as 1918, Pound was saying that Browning's *Sordello* was "the best long poem in English since Chaucer." It is the saga of a thirteenth-century Italian troubadour, who figures in Dante's *Inferno*; a vast historical tapestry that runs to 160 pages of somewhat constipated rhymed couplets.

> Who will, may hear Sordello's story told;
> His story? Who believes me shall behold
> The man, pursue his fortunes to the end,
> Like me . . .

Can anyone read the whole poem now? But Pound found many wonders in it. He admired Browning particularly for the invention of the dramatic monologue, a form that he transmuted to his own *personae* (masks), a means for giving a poem a speaking voice that was not his own. "Marvoil," in which he impersonates the troubadour Arnaut de Mareuil, is a good example.

Sordello

As Pound began to plan the *Cantos* he believed he would need a *persona* for them. His choice was Sordello. The first *Cantos* to be published was a draft of 1–3 in *Poetry* magazine in 1917. They were totally different from the final versions of 1925, both in content and style. Poundians call them the *Ur-Cantos*.[2] *Ur-Canto* 1 begins:

> Hang it all, there can be but one "Sordello,"
> But say I want to, say I take your whole bag of tricks,
> Let in your quirks and tweeks, and say the thing's an art-form,
> Your "Sordello," and that the "modern world"
> Needs such a rag-bag to stuff all its thoughts in;
> Say that I dump my catch, shiny and silvery
> As fresh sardines flapping and slipping on the marginal cobbles?

These lines are not in the lovely melopoeic cadences of the revised and later cantos. They are jerky and tentative. It's unfortunate that Pound spoke of a "rag-bag" in the first *Ur-Canto*. Ever since, his detractors have been saying that the *Cantos* too have no proper structure and are indeed a "rag-bag" into which he stuffed everything that he knew, saw, read, heard, or remembered. This is not so. There is a structure, but it is extremely intricate and hard to discern. At some point, Pound concluded that a single mask-voice would not do the job for him. The revised Canto 1 has a single voice, that of Odysseus going down to the underworld, the *nekuia*, but soon the poem becomes polyphonic (as well as polylingual) with many voices collaged closely together. As Hugh Kenner explains it, the poem becomes a "mental kaleidoscope ('the phantasticon') . . . The man talking [gives] place to rapidly dissolving images."

Poor Sordello! He got the heave-ho. But he still has three lines at the beginning of the revised Canto 2, and, perhaps to make amends, Pound gives him what sounds like some pleasant fornication in Canto 29: "And Sordello subtracted her from that husband/ And lay with her in Tarviso . . ."

Pavannes

What a poet writes in his youth is never entirely lost. Many of Dylan Thomas's greatest lines came from the notebook he kept in school. Did Pound salvage anything or learn anything from "The Water-butt"? Nothing of substance. But in matters of verbal tone and style there may have been survivals. A good place to look is in the collection of pieces in lighter vein, *Pavannes and Divagations*, which he put together when he was "a guest of the government" in St. Elizabeths Hospital in 1958.

Pound refused all offers from publishers to write his autobiography. He told me: "When a man writes his meemoirs that's a sign that he's finished." But in 1923 he published *Indiscretions,* a fifty-page account of the lives of his progenitors which is a delightful social document, full of witty Ezratic confabulations. Later, it was included in the *Pavannes and Divagations* collection. All of the family names are changed. Pound's father, Homer, is Rip Weight; his mother is Hermione. There is a colorful Uncle Euripides out in Wisconsin, while Ezra refers to himself as "the infant Gargantua." The style has little nips of Henry James, whom Pound read attentively, but I think I also hear in it a touch of the cantering pace of "The Water-butt":

> Before the birth of the infant Gargantua, the great elephant Sampson broke loose from the travelling circus, and upset the lion cages and chased his keeper out of the tent; and his keeper jumped on his cayoos and put for the railroad siding, and you could have seen the cowboys out after it, letting off their six-shooters into its rear.

Also in *Pavannes* is the tale of *Jodindranath Mawhwor*:

> The soul of Jodindranath Mawhwor clove to the God of this universe and he meditated the law of the Shastras. . . .
>
> Jodindranath rose in the morning and brushed his teeth, after having performed other unavoidable duties as prescribed in the sutra, and he applied to his body a not excessive, as he considered it, amount of unguents and perfumes. He then blackened his eyebrows, drew faint lines under his eyes, put a fair deal of rouge on his lips, and regarded himself in the mirror. Then having chewed a few betel leaves to perfume his breath, and munched another bonne-bouche of perfume, he set about his day's business.

Fairly close, I think, to the arch intonation of "The Water-butt." The "Frivolities" section of *Pavannes* exhibits various strains of Pound's humor. The one that relates most in tone to "The Water-butt" is "Our Contemporaries":

> When the Taihaitian princess
> Heard that he had decided,
> She rushed out into the sunlight and swarmed up a
>   cocoanut palm tree,
>
> But he returned to this island
> And wrote ninety Petrarchan sonnets.

Redondillas

A more ambitious poem whose tone may connect remotely with "The Water-butt" is "Redondillas, or Something of that Sort." Pound had the poem set up by Elkin Mathews as part of his London book *Canzoni* of 1911. But when he saw it in proof he decided that it was insufficiently serious and withdrew it. Fifty-four years later, when the text surfaced in the Humanities Research Center at Texas, he allowed me to publish it, but with the stipulation that it appear only in a limited edition.

> I would sing the American people,
>> God send them some civilization;
> I would sing of the nations of Europe,
>> God grant them some method of cleansing
> The fetid extent of their evils.
>> I would sing of my love "To-morrow,"
> But Yeats has written an essay,
>> Why should I stop to repeat it?
> I don't like this hobbledy metre,
>> but find it easy to write in,
> I would sing to the tune of *"Mi platz"*
>> were it not for the trouble of rhyming,
> Besides, not six men believe me
>> when I sing in a beautiful measure.
>
> I demonstrate the breadth of my vision.
>> I am bored by this talk of the tariff,
> I too have heard of T. Roosevelt.
>> I have met with the "Common Man,"
> I admit that he usually bores me,
>> He is usually stupid or smug.

The *redondilla* is a sixteenth-century octosyllabic quatrain, which Pound would have known from his college studies, but he does not follow it here. The bouncing "hobbledy metre," as he calls it, is not one that he used in any other poem.

The Archaisms

Pound loved them, perhaps out of reverence for the past. In the first poem of *Personae*, "The Tree," which he wrote for his Bryn Mawr sweetheart Hilda Doolittle (later to become, at his fiat, the first Imagist poet, H.D.) we find:

> Of Daphne and the laurel bow
> And that god-feasting couple old
> That grew elm-oak amid the wold.

Archaic words kept turning up until Ford gave him a dressing down about it, and even sometimes after that. In Canto 1 of 1925 he still writes "I dug the ell-square pitkin" and "Stand from the fosse, leave me my bloody bever/ For soothsay." The archaisms are really most disconcerting in the translations of troubadour *cansos* and the sonnets of the Italian poets of the *dolce stil nuovo* where he had to use them to find enough rhyming sounds for the extremely complicated rhyme schemes.

> Death who art haught, the wretched's remedy,
> Grace! Grace! hands joined I do beseech it thee,
> Come, see and conquer for worse things on me
> Are launched by love. My senses that did live,
>
> Consumèd are and quenched, and e'en in this place
> Where I was galliard, now I see that I am
> Fallen away, and where my steps I misplace,
> Fall pain and grief; to open tears I nigh am.

> CAVALCANTI : *Sonetto XXXIII*

Undergraduate Humor

I asked my guru, Professor A. Walton Litz, about "The Water-butt." "What is this, anyway?" "It's undergraduate humor," he said, "the brightest kid in the class showing off that he has read things." "What things? Is it any particular parody?" "Hard to say . . . but at that time Booth Tarkington was in the air." In one of the letters to his parents in 1907 Pound reports that he had been reading Gilbert Parker, a Canadian author who was then popular.[3]

Campus high spirits. Fun and games with word play. Let's be outrageous. Let's reach for esoteric words and twist them to make them ludicrous. Flamboyance. Pomposity. An *absurdité voulue*. Fancy punning. Some highbrow camp that descends to kitsch. And what did Nabokov mean by *poshlust*? I had classmates at Harvard who wrote in such ways, though most often they got published in the *Lampoon*, not sedate Mother *Advocate*.

Pound was unusual in that he never outgrew the youthful kidding, at least in his letters. Those extraordinary letters—I know of nothing like them. Nearly to the end of his life his letters were full of high jinx and teasing. This is at its most brilliant in his correspondence with Eliot, soon to be published I hope. The zany salutations in the letters to Old Possum set the tone:

> "Waal, now me deer protopheriius . . ."
> "To the affbl Protopgerius Wunkus . . ."
> "Waaal Possum, my fine ole Marse Supial . . ."
> "Waaal my able an sable old Crepuscule . . ."

The letter of April 25, 1936, to Eliot shows the Kollitch Komedian in fine form:

> NO!! my dear Sathanas: On reflection I see that it wd. be whoredom, and not even en grande cocotte.
>
> If the luminous reason of one's criticism iz that one shd. focus attention on what deserves it, a note by E.P. on Bridges wd. be a falsification of values.
>
> I thought (cogitation, the aimless flitter before arriving at meditatio) that the cadaver might be used to feed young pelicans, or to do honour to the obese but meritorious F.[4]
>
> But more I fink ov it, the less honest does such a wangle appear.

It is not a case where one can merely throw Richardly Alding-
tonian dirt. I can't think Britsches has enough influence to be
worth attacking. I mean one hasn't the excuse, as one has with
nine-tenths of your *Criterion* writers, all Murrays, ----, bastards,
Normans, Angells, etc., that the vipers ought to be killed. The
number of putrid pigs in England is so large that to dig up a
corpse for reburial, especially a corpse of the null, wd. be inexcusable unless one were absolootly in need of feed within the
fortnight.

I did not instantly expect to find the EVIL one lurking under yr.
weskit. But so was it. -/-/

It was a special delight for Pound's correspondents when he
enclosed a doggerel poem in a letter. This to Eliot in 1937, about
Djuna Barnes:

> There onct wuzza lady named Djuna
> Who wrote rather like a baboon. Her
> Blubbery prose had no fingers or toes
> And we wish Whale had found this out sooner.[5]

Another one, called "Xmas Owed," was written to me in 1935
on the occasion of Anthony Eden's marriage to a banker's
daughter.[6] To Ezra, of course, the sum of evil was a banker.

> Pretty Tony, the beauty's son,
> Married a bank and up he run.
> Hickery, dickery, dickery dock
> Let young men die for my bank stock.

Who was Geofry Stowell, with whose name Pound signed
"In the Water-butt"? None of my Poundian friends have ever
heard of him. But it's a genteel, almost Jamesian name, which
would have gone down well in Wyncote, where Pound's parents were stalwarts of Calvary Presbyterian Church.

Hang it all, Robert Browning, there can be but the one Ezra!

MOTZ EL SON

*Some Notes on Pound's
Medieval Translations*

About ten years ago a young scholar, Charlotte Ward, who was working on the manuscripts of Pound's Provençal translations in the Pound archive at the Beinecke Library at Yale, found a group of poems that Pound had not included in his collection of *Translations*. Some were variant versions of poems he did publish, early drafts; some he probably thought not up to his best standard; others he may simply have filed away and forgotten about. Since these texts had not had his imprimatur, it seemed appropriate to make no large claims for them but to publish them in a limited edition for scholars and collectors. The great handprinter K. K. Merker of The Windhover Press at the University of Iowa produced a book which is a masterpiece of fine bookmaking. It was published in 1985 and is entitled *Forked Branches*. At Merker's invitation I did a short introduction which I have now expanded to give some fuller treatment of Pound's passionate interest in the troubadours. *Motz el son*. (Words as song.) That is the key phrase for the work of the poets of Provence from the eleventh to the thirteenth century. Pound studied and translated them for over twenty years.

From his youth, Pound was a prodigious reader and it seems likely that he was reading troubadour poetry before he went to college. He began writing poetry at fifteen. But his intensive study of the language of Provence, in which the troubadours wrote their poems, began at Hamilton College in 1903 under the tutelage of Professor William Pierce Shepard of the Department of Romance Languages. Some thirty years later, he paid tribute to Shepard in a letter to another Hamilton professor:

> Bill shep gave me the Provençal. There was no Provençal course, and I cdn't have paid him. I mean 'GAVE.'

Encouraged by Shepard, Pound began to translate Provençal poetry. One of his first efforts, "Belangal Alba," appeared in the *Hamilton Literary Magazine* in 1905. (It reappears in 1909 in his London book *Personae* in a revised version under the title "Alba Belingalis," where Pound adds a note that this may be the oldest fragment of Provençal verse known to survive.[1] *Alba* means dawn in Provençal but is also the name of a verse form referring to the parting of lovers at dawn.)

From Hamilton, Pound returned to the University of Pennsylvania for graduate study. Here again, he had the good fortune to find a learned and inspiring mentor: Dr. Hugo Rennert, Professor of Romance Languages and author of a life of Lope de Vega. Pound left Dr. Rennert's seminar in Provençal with a love of the language and its poetry, which was to become an obsession for the rest of his life.

Another influence was Justin H. Smith's *The Troubadours at Home* (1899). Smith was an English amateur who trekked through Provence locating old troubadour castles, many of them in ruins. He did charming pen and ink sketches of what he saw, and wrote about the troubadours with fervor, quoting liberally from their poems and from the *vidas*, the apocryphal brief lives written by the editors of posthumous collections.

Pound became convinced that the poetic art of the troubadours was as subtle a technique for verse as had ever been devised. He was intrigued by the way the length and weight of words were blended with the music to which the poems were sung, and the complicated rhyme schemes with their echo effects (the *motz el son*). He set out to learn all he could about the poetry of Provence, constantly revising and refining his translations. There are seven different versions of one poem by Arnaut

Daniel in the Yale archive. It may well be that Pound's love of Provençal and of the early poetry in the other Romance languages had something to do with his decision to leave the United States to live in Europe, first in Venice and then in Paris, London, and various parts of Italy.

In Canto 20, Pound tells of a trip to Germany to consult the great scholar Emil Lévy about a word he had been unable to find in the dictionaries:

> And that year I went up to Freiburg,
> And Rennert had said: Nobody, no, nobody
> Knows anything about Provençal, or if there is anybody,
> It's old Lévy."
> . . .
> And I went to old Lévy, and it was by then 6.30
> in the evening, and he trailed half way across Freiburg
> before dinner, to see the two strips of copy,
> Arnaut's, settant'uno R. superiore (Ambrosiana)
> Not that I could sing him the music.
> And he said: Now is there anything I can tell you?"
> And I said: I dunno, sir, or
> "Yes, Doctor, what do they mean by *noigandres*?"
> And he said: 'Noigandres! NOIgandres!
> "You know for seex mon's of my life
> "Effery night when I go to bett, I say to myself:
> "Noigandres, eh, *noi*gandres,
> "Now what the DEFFIL can that mean!"

(Pound does not tell us in the poem, but Lévy eventually reached a conclusion about *noigandres*, that it is two words run together and means "banishes sadness.")

In the winter of 1909–10, Pound was invited to give a series of lectures on "The Development of Literature in Southern Europe" at the Regent Street Polytechnic in London, and the following year another series on "Medieval Literature." (The tuition for each course was seven shillings and sixpence.) These lectures were at first based on his notes from Dr. Rennert's seminar; but when his first prose book, *The Spirit of Romance*, was published in 1910, it included many new insights from his current research and many new translations.

The Spirit of Romance, which has as its subtitle "An Attempt to Define Somewhat the Charm of the Pre-Renaissance Literature of Latin Europe," ranges far beyond the poetry of the troubadours. The book embraces the background of the transition from Latin to the Romance languages, the medieval poetry of Northern France, the *Chanson de Roland*, Dante and his precursors, such as Guinizelli and Cavalcanti, the Spanish epic of *El Cid*, Renaissance Latin poems, Villon, the plays of Lope de Vega, and Camoens's Portuguese epic *The Lusiads*. We can learn much about the troubadour poets Pound translated from the second, third, and fifth chapters of *The Spirit of Romance*, from which I quote at random.

> [In the twelfth century] the Troubadours were melting the common tongue and fashioning it into new harmonies depending not upon the alternation of quantities but upon rhyme and accent.

The troubadours did not know that they were writing in "Provençal." That term came later. For them, their language was *langue d'oc* (whence the province of that name), while the poets of Northern France, the trouvères, who wrote the *chansons de geste*, were using *langue d'oil*, *oc* and *oil* being the Southern and Northern versions of what would become the French *oui*— "yes." (In *Personae* Pound has a fine little sequence of Provençal adaptations entitled "Langue d'oc.")

Provençal is also called Occitan and to this day there is an Occitan cultural movement in the south of France. Peasants in the Dordogne speak a dialect of Occitan. Frédéric Mistral wrote an impressive quasi-epic, *Mirèio*, in Occitan in 1859, which won him the Nobel Prize in 1904, and there is an active school of poets around Béziers writing in the language today.

Arnaut Daniel and Bertran de Born

In *The Spirit of Romance* Pound wrote:

> The Twelfth Century . . . has left us two perfect gifts: the church of
> San Zeno in Verona and the Canzoni of Arnaut Daniel . . .

Arnaut Daniel (1180–1210) was Pound's favorite among the
Provençal poets. There are eight translations of his work in
Forked Branches. The influence of Daniel is evident in Pound's
book of poetry *Provença* (1910), there is a fine essay on him in
Pound's *Literary Essays* (1954), and the final versions of his
translations are available in the *Translations* volume (1953).
Pound was not the first to recognize Daniel's greatness. Petrarch
called him the *"gran maestro d'amor* [the master of chivalric love-
lore] who still doth honor to his native land by his fair, fine-
wrought speech." Dante also knew the poetry of the troubadours. In Canto 26 of the *Purgatorio* he has the poet Guinizelli
tell him "This one whom I point out with my finger [Daniel] was
the better craftsman [*il miglior fabbro*] in the mother tongue. He
surpassed all verses of love and prose of romances . . ." Seven
centuries later, this historic phrase would reappear when T. S.
Eliot dedicated *The Waste Land* to Pound as *il miglior fabbro*.

In his own time, Bertran de Born (c. 1140–c. 1214) was called a
"lover of strife for strife's sake." He paid for it. In the Malebolge
of Hell, Dante met him, a headless trunk carrying in his hand
his severed head, which he swung like a lantern. When Dante
called out to him, the head responded:

> Behold the pain grievous, thou who, breathing goest looking
> upon the dead; see if there be pain great as this is, and that thou
> may'st bear tidings of me, know me, Bertrans de Born; who gave
> never comfort to the young king. I made the father and the son
> rebels between them; Achithophel made not more of Absalom
> and David by his ill-wandering goads. Because I have sundered
> persons so joined (in kinship), I bear my brain parted.

(The "young king" was Henry II Plantagenet, brother of Richard Coeur de Lion, who was fighting in the Dordogne to lay hold on territory he claimed from his marriage to Eleanor of Aquitaine. Bertran regretted killing him in battle. Pound translated Bertran's poem of grief for his opponent in the "Planh for the Young English King" in *Personae*.)

Bernart de Ventadorn and Jaufre Rudel[2]

The *vida* of Bernart de Ventadorn (1150–80) tells us that:

> Becoming a "fair man and skilled," and knowing how to make poetry, and being courteous and learned, he is honored by the Viscount of Ventadorn; makes songs to the Countess; makes one or two songs too many to the Countess; with the sequel of a Countess under lock and key, and one more troubadour wandering from court to court, and ending his days at the monastery of Dalon.

> At this time (1126–70) lived Jaufre Rudel, Prince of Blaia, whose love for the Countess of Tripoli has been resung by so many.

Barbara Smythe tells a bit more about Rudel in her *Troubadour Poets* (1911):

> Jaufre Rudel of Blaye was a very noble man, the Prince of Blaye. And he fell in love with the Countess of Tripoli, whom he had never seen, because of the praise that he had heard said of her by the pilgrims who came from Antioch; and he made many songs about her, with good melodies and few words. And for the sake of her he took the Cross and set out to sea. And on the voyage a grievous illness fell upon him, so that those who were in the ship with him thought he was dead, but they brought him to Tripoli and carried him to an inn, thinking him dead. And it was made known to the Countess, and she came to him and took him in her arms, and he knew she was the Countess, and recovered con-

sciousness, and praised God and thanked him for letting him live
to see her. And so he died in the lady's arms. And she had him
honorably buried in the Church of the Templars, and on the same
day she became a nun, through the grief that she felt by reason of
his death.

Arnaut de Mareuil

One of the finest poems in Pound's *Personae*, where he is writing
under the mask of another person, is "Marvoil."

> A poor clerk I, "Arnaut the less" they call me,
> And because I have small mind to sit
> Day long, long day cooped on a stool
> A-jumbling o' figures for Maître Jacques Polin,
> I ha' taken to rambling the South here.
>
> The Vicomte de Bezier's not such a bad lot.
> I made rimes to his lady this three year:
> Vers and canzone, till that damn'd son of Aragon,
> Alfonso the half-bald, took to hanging
> *His* helmet at Beziers. . . .

The man of whom Pound is speaking is the troubadour he called
Arnaut de Marvoil, though Mareuil is the usual spelling. He
lived in the last third of the twelfth century. In *Proensa* (1978),
one of the best collections of Provençal translations done since
Pound's, Paul Blackburn, translating Mareuil's *vida*, writes:

> Arnaut de Mareuil was from the bishopric of Périgord, from a
> castle called Mareuil, and was a clerk of poor extraction. Because
> he could make no living from his education, he went out into the
> world, for he was intelligent and knew trobar [writing songs]
> well. The stars and his luck led him to the court of the countess of
> Burlatz who was the daughter of the valorous count Raimon and
> the wife of the viscount of Beziers who was named Talliafero.
> This Arnaut was a very handsome and well-built man, sang

well and read in the vernacular. And the countess was very good to him, granting him favors and honor. He fell in love with her and made cansos for her, but did not dare to tell her, or anyone else, the name of the one who had written them. He said, rather, that someone else had made them.

But as it happened, love forced him so hard that he made a canso, the one that begins "La franca captenensa," and in this canso he reveals to her the love that he had for her. The countess did not discourage him, but heard and accepted his pleas and found them agreeable. She outfitted him with some handsome clothes, granted him great honor, and gave him the boldness he needed to compose for her. He came to be a highly respected man in the court and made many good cansos for the countess, which songs disclose that he had great good of her and great pain.

But Arnaut's good fortune did not last. Alfonso of Aragon became the wooer of the countess, and she sent her troubadour away from court, as Pound dramatises in his poem.

Sordello

In giving us Sordello's *vida*, Pound adds comments on Robert Browning's treatment of the story. When Pound began planning the *Cantos* he thought he might employ Sordello as the poem's main speaking voice.

Sordello was of Mantuan Territory of Sirier, son of a poor cavalier who had name Sier Escort [Browning's El Corte], and he delighted himself in chançons, to learn and to make them. And he mingled with the good men of the court. And he learned all that he could and made coblas and sirventes. And he came thence to the court of St Bonifaci, and the Count honoured him much. And he fell in love with the wife of the Count, in the form of pleasure (*a forma de solatz*), and she with him. [The Palma of Browning's poem and the Cunizza of Dante's.] And it befell that the Count stood ill with her brothers. And thus he estranged himself from her and from Sier Sceillme and Sier Albrics. Thus her brothers caused her to be stolen from the Count by Sier Sordello and the latter came to stop with them. And he [Sordello] stayed a long time with them in great happiness, and then he went into Pro-ensa where he received great honours from all the good men and from the Count and from the Countess who gave him a good castle and a wife of gentle birth. [Browning with perfect right alters the ending to suit his purpose.]

The Italian Poets

We come now to the Italian poets. A few of them are in *Forked Branches* but the greater part are in *Translations*. Francesco Petrarch (1304–74) holds rank among the greatest Italian writers. I am surprised that Pound translated him—it must have been very early on—because later Pound thought poorly of Petrarch. In his essay "Medievalism," he compared him to Guido Cavalcanti thus:

> In that art [poetry] the gulf between Petrarch's capacity and Guido's is the great gulf, not of degree, but of kind. In Guido the "figure," the strong metamorphic or "picturesque" expression is there with purpose to convey or to interpret a definite meaning. In Petrarch it is ornament, the prettiest ornament he could find, but not an irreplaceable ornament, or one that he couldn't have used just about as well somewhere else. In fact he very often does use it, and them, somewhere, and nearly everywhere, else, all over the place.

In Canto 73, one of the two "missing Cantos," which were written in Italian and have not yet been published in English, Pound, like Dante, visits the infernal regions and there meets a horseman who is the Florentine poet Guido Cavalcanti (1250?–1300?). They engage in conversation, and Cavalcanti tells Pound:

> I am that Guido you loved
> > both for my spirit's pride
> and clarity of judgment.

The greeting is fitting because Cavalcanti was the Italian poet whose work Pound loved best, next to that of Dante. When in 1912 Pound published *The Sonnets and Ballate of Guido Cavalcanti*, in the introduction he wrote:

> Than Guido Cavalcanti no psychologist of the emotion is more keen in his understanding, more precise in his expression; we have in him no rhetoric, but always a true description, whether it be of pain itself, or of the apathy that comes when the emotions and possibilities of emotion are exhausted, or of that stranger state when the feeling by its intensity surpasses our power of bearing and we seem to stand aside and watch it surging across some thing or being with whom we are no longer identified.

Pound admired Cavalcanti for the precision of his intellect and lamented that "we appear to have lost the radiant world where one thought cuts through another with clean edge" of the Middle Ages. Cavalcanti, who was a friend of Dante, and a master of the *dolce stil nuovo*, ("the sweet new style," which was emerging from dialect into literary language in Tuscany), is said to have persuaded Dante to write the *Divine Comedy* in the vernacular rather than in Latin. They, too, exchanged sonnets. One of the loveliest of them is the "Guido vorrei che tu e Lapo ed io . . ." by Dante, which Rossetti translates:

> Guido, I wish that Lapo, thou and I,   [Lapo Gianni]
>   Could be by spells convey'd, as it were now,
>   Upon a barque, with all the winds that blow
> Across all seas at our good will to hie.
> So no mischance nor temper of the sky
>   Should mar our course with spite or cruel slip;
>   But we, observing old companionship,
> To be companions still should long thereby.
> And Lady Joan, and Lady Beatrice,
>   And her the thirtieth on my roll, with us
>   Should our good wizard set, o'er seas to move
>   And not to talk of anything but love:

And they three ever to be well at ease
As we should be, I think, if this were thus.

It is fascinating how a great line of poetry will travel down through the centuries. Thus Cavalcanti's "Perch'io non spero di tornar gia mai" was to become T. S. Eliot's "Because I do not hope to turn again" in *Ash Wednesday*. And a phrase of Cavalcanti's that is repeated several times in the later *Cantos*, and with particular poignancy in *The Pisan Cantos*, when Pound was held in a cage in the Army's Disciplinary Training Center near Pisa and had nothing to live with but his memories, is Cavalcanti's "In quella parte/ dove sta memoria." ("Where memory liveth...")[3]

Pound had Cavalcanti with him all his life. He wrote a number of essays about him (one of which is in the *Literary Essays*). In 1932 he published privately his own edition of his work, the *Guido Cavalcanti Rime*, with variorum readings from the different texts and many photographs of the manuscripts from which he had worked in Italian libraries. Pound continually revised his translations of Cavalcanti. I think there are at least four successive versions of the great poem "Donna mi pregha," the last one appearing as Canto 36, which begins:

A lady asks me
I speak in season
She seeks reason for an affect, wild often
That is so proud he hath Love for a name
Who denys it can hear the truth now
Wherefore I speak to the present knowers
Having no hope that low-hearted
Can bring sight to such reason
Be there not natural demonstration
I have no will to try proof-bringing
Or say where it hath birth
What is its virtu and power
Its being and every moving

Or delight whereby 'tis called "to love"
Or if man can show it to sight.

In "Donna mi pregha" 52 out of every 154 syllables are bound together in tonal patterns. My colleague at Brown, Tony Oldcorn, professor of Italian literature, cautions that in translating the poem Pound took too much from Aristotle and the Scholastics and too little from the Neo-Platonists. I record Tony's warning without comment, except to recall a savant named Kretschmer whom I read in my youth who said that "Unsere ganze Philosophie ist eine Berichtigung des Sprachgebrauches." (All philosophy is correction of linguistic usage.)

Some passages from *The Spirit of Romance* illuminate how Provençal poetry merged into the *dolce stil nuovo* of the Italians:

> In the later Provençal forms the stanzas were usually, though not always, more simple . . . and the rhymes of the first stanza were usually retained throughout the poem; thus each succeeding stanza was an echo not only of the order but of the terminal sounds of the first.
>
> An effect of one of Arnaut Daniel's canzoni is that of a chord struck repeatedly in crescendo. The sound-beauty of the Italian canzone depends on the variations of the rhymes.
>
> The Provençal canzone can be understood when sung. Tuscan canzoni often require close study in print before they will yield their meaning. But after one knows the meaning, their exquisite sound spoken, or sung, is most enjoyable.
>
> . . . The cult of Provence had been a cult of the emotions; and with it there had been some, hardly conscious, study of emotional psychology. In Tuscany the cult is a cult of the harmonies of the mind. If one is in sympathy with this form of objective imagination and this quality of vision, there is no poetry which has such enduring, such if I may say so, indestructible charm.
>
> The best poetry of this time appeals by its truth, by its subtlety, and by its refined exactness.

Walking Tours

Pound's attachment to Provence was not solely a bookish one. He loved the country itself and made two vacation walking tours in the Dordogne, searching for the castles and towns where his beloved troubadours had lived, most of them, alas, now abandoned. His impressions of the first trip in 1912 are recorded in the poem "Provincia Deserta" (*Personae*):

> At Rochecoart,
> Where the hills part
> > in three ways,
> And three valleys, full of winding roads,
> Fork out to south and north,
> There is a place of trees . . . gray with lichen.
> I have walked there
> > thinking of old days.
> At Chalais
> > is a pleached arbour;
> Old pensioners and old protected women
> Have the right there —
> > it is charity.
> I have crept over old rafters,
> > peering down
> Over the Dronne,
> > over a stream full of lilies.
> Eastward the road lies,
> > Aubeterre is eastward,
> With a garrulous old man at the inn.
> I know the roads in that place:
> Mareuil to the north-east,
> > La Tour,
> There are three keeps near Mareuil,
> And an old woman,
> > glad to hear Arnaut,
> Glad to lend one dry clothing.

I have walked
            into Perigord,
I have seen the torch-flames, high-leaping,
Painting the front of that church;
Heard, under the dark, whirling laughter.
I have looked back over the stream
                and seen the high building,
Seen the long minarets, the white shafts.
I have gone in Riberac
                and in Sarlat,
I have climbed rickety stairs, heard talk of Croy,
Walked over En Bertran's old layout,
Have seen Narbonne, and Cahors, and Chalus,
Have seen Excideuil, carefully fashioned.

I have said:
            "Here such a one walked.
"Here Coeur-de-Lion was slain.
            "Here was good singing.
"Here one man hastened his step.
            "Here one lay panting."
I have looked south from Hautefort,
            thinking of Montaignac, southward.
I have lain in Rocafixada,
            level with sunset,
Have seen the copper come down
            tingeing the mountains,
I have seen the fields, pale, clear as an emerald,
Sharp peaks, high spurs, distant castles.
I have said: "The old roads have lain here.
"Men have gone by such and such valleys
"Where the great halls were close together."
I have seen Foix on its rock, seen Toulouse, and
            Arles greatly altered,
I have seen the ruined "Dorata."
            I have said:

"Riquier! Guido."
      I have thought of the second Troy,
Some little prized place in Auvergnat:
Two men tossing a coin, one keeping a castle,
One set on the highway to sing.
      He sang a woman.
Auvergne rose to the song;
      The Dauphin backed him.

"The castle to Austors!"
      "Pieire kept the singing—
"A fair man and a pleasant."
      He won the lady,
Stole her away for himself, kept her against armed
      force:
So ends that story.
That age is gone;
Pieire de Maensac is gone.
I have walked over these roads;
I have thought of them living.

During his walking trip of 1912 Pound also kept a rough jour-
nal, often written on the back of hotel stationery. He recorded
what he was doing, made rough draft translations of Provençal
poems he liked, and blocked out theories about troubadour poetry. It was rather disorganized, but the original pages have been
preserved in the Pound archive at Beinecke Library, Yale. Many
years later he thought of turning it into a short book but found
the work too taxing. It has now been deciphered by Richard
Sieburth (New York University) and the best parts will be included in Sieburth's book *Ezra Pound in France,* to be published
by New Directions in 1989.

In his preliminary report Sieburth writes: "The text is rather a
jigaw puzzle and has dull stretches, but it shows Pound in 1912
beginning to try to get his eye on the object and attempting
sheerly descriptive prose.... It will be valuable for study of E.P.
as a *landscape* poet. The attention to light and color points forward

to the *Cantos* (as does the whole notion of Troy in Provence). On July 16, 1912, Pound notes: "now should I be finally equipped for the indicting [sic] of true pastorals."

Pound's longest walking tour in Provence was made in the spring and summer of 1919 when he was accompanied by his wife Dorothy, and, for part of the time, by T. S. Eliot. Among other "sacred sites," they visited Toulouse, Foix, Montréjeau, Thiviers, Excideuil, Brive, Mauléon, Hautefort, Rocamadour, Clermont-Ferrand, Montignac, and Brantôme. A fairly detailed record of this trip exists through the postcards the Pounds wrote Dorothy's parents in London. Omar Pound has given me permission to quote from them. (A full itinerary of this trip will be found in Philip Grover's *The London Years*, 1908–1920, AMC Press, 1978.)

> (*from Rocamadour, August 5, 1919, D.P.*)
> We came over the hills across gorgeous bare scrub, stirring up 1000's of butterflies from a town on the Dordogne.
> This is a place of pilgrimage, since all time — and there are black Virgins and a miraculous bell and 200 something steps up the village, that they crawl up on their knees in Sept: full of tourists devout and otherwise — but a really amazing place all tucked against the huge rock...

> (*from Montignac, August 2, 1919, D.P.*)
> We spent last night at Altaforte — & started out soon after 6 a.m. . . . .
> It was a lovely walk, about 16 miles over highish hills. — This was where Bertrand de Born's "Maint" lived. — Last night we slept close to where Henry II's men probably camped, besieging B. de Born...

> (*from Brantôme, August 18, 1919, E.P.*)
> Brantôme reached & pleasing. T. [Tom Eliot] has 7 blisters. Will probably proceed by train tomorrow...

Hidden Meanings

Peter Makin in *Provence and Pound* (which is the indispensable book on the subject) tells us that Pound built up a myth which assumed something was "behind" the troubadours, that is a philosophical or even a mystical position. "Pound was struggling with two opposing approaches." One view is that the poets in Provence and later in Tuscany (Cavalcanti et al.) were writing secrets into their work. *Trobar clus*, the "closed song" of Arnaut Daniel is thought to have hidden meanings. The lady who is being praised might stand for a religious sect. Whereas "the other view was far more difficult, but was more natural to Pound's temperament: that the *psychology* of the poetry represented a world-view which could quite naturally be acted out in the form of a ritual; so that the terms of the poetry were not code-words, but represented actual personal situations."

Let us let Pound himself set forth some of his esoteric theories with quotations from the "Psychology and the Troubadours" chapter in *The Spirit of Romance*.

> Behind the narratives is a comparatively simple state of "romanticism," behind the canzos, the "love code."
>
> The "chivalric love," was as I understand it, an art, that is to say a religion. The writers of "trobar clus" did not seek obscurity for the sake of obscurity. . . . The second sort of canzone is a ritual. It must be conceived and approached as ritual. It has its purpose and its effect. These are different from those of simple song. They are perhaps subtler. They make their revelations to those who are already expert.
>
> Consider the history of the time, the Albigensian Crusade, nominally against a sect tinged with Manichean heresy, and remember how Provençal song is never wholly disjunct from pagan rites of May Day. Provence was less disturbed than the rest of Europe by invasion from the North in the darker ages; if paganism survived anywhere it would have been, unofficially, in the Langue d'Oc. That the spirit was, in Provence, Hellenic is seen readily enough by anyone who will compare the *Greek Anthology*

with the work of the troubadours. They have, in some way, lost the names of the gods and remembered the names of lovers. Ovid and *The Eclogues* of Virgil would seem to have been their chief documents.

The question is: Did this "close ring," this aristocracy of emotion, evolve, out of its half memories of Hellenistic mysteries, a cult—a cult stricter, or more subtle, than that of the celibate ascetics, a cult for the purgation of the soul by a refinement of, and lordship over, the senses? . . .

Did this "chivalric love," this exotic, take on mediumistic properties? Stimulated by the color or quality of emotion, did that "color" take on forms interpretive of the divine order? Did it lead to an "exteriorization of the sensibility," and interpretation of the cosmos by feeling?

We are a fair distance from Catullus when we come to Peire Vidal's: "Good Lady, I think I see God when I gaze on your delicate body."

Richard St. Victor has left us one very beautiful passage on the splendors of paradise. They are ineffable and innumerable and no man having beheld them can fittingly narrate them or even remember them exactly. Nevertheless by naming over all the most beautiful things we know we may draw back upon the mind some vestige of the heavenly splendor.

A Light from Eleusis

Speaking of the catalogue poems, where the troubadour enumerates his beloved's beauties and virtues, Pound suggests that "the Lady serves as a sort of *mantram*."

In his little "Credo" of 1930, Pound wrote "I believe that a light from Eleusis persisted throughout the middle ages and set beauty in the song of Provence and of Italy." The following year in "Terra Italica" (*Selected Prose*), he stated that "the cult of Eleusis will explain not only general phenomena but particular beauties in Arnaut Daniel or in Guido Cavalcanti." He went further to declare that "Eleusis contains the summation of concentration of the wisdoms [of every branch of knowledge]." We are to believe that somehow the spirit and perhaps even the erotic rituals of the Eleusinian Mysteries survived underground through the Roman imperium and the Dark Ages to reappear and flourish in Provence in the cult of *amor*. Here the indispensable book is Leon Surette's *A Light from Eleusis,* which demonstrates how the rites of Eleusis may be seen as one of several possible paradigms for the action of the *Cantos.* What were these mysteries which were so important to Pound that they became a leitmotif in the *Cantos?* Surette explains:

> At Eleusis the candidates descended a few steps into the Telesterion or inner temple in order to take part in the nocturnal celebration of the sacred mysteries. In the temple the hierophant would preside over the *epopteia,* or "showing forth", which must have been some kind of theophany, accompanied by a great fire. The Mysteries are based upon the myth of the rape of Persephone by Pluto—or, perhaps more accurately, the myth serves to explain in a veiled manner the nature of the Mysteries. The principal divinities are Demeter, her daughter, Persephone, whose mystic name is Koré (daughter), and Pluto or chthonic Dionysus (or father Zagreus and son Zagreus, husband and child of Persephone). Hermes as psychopomp and messenger, also has a role in the ritual. . . .

The best account we have of this mystical (but to Pound also erotic) experience is attributed to Plutarch:

> [There are] chance directions, difficult detours, disquieting and endless walks through the darkness. Then, before the end, complete terror; one is overcome by shivering, trembling and breaks out into a cold sweat. But then a marvelous light bursts before one's eyes, and one walks in pure meadows where voices echo and figures dance. Sacred words and divine apparitions inspire a religious respect. At that time, the man, from then perfect and initiated, becomes free and holy and moving about without restraint celebrates the Mysteries, a crown on his head. He lives

with pure and holy men, and sees on earth the crowd of those
who are not initiated and purified, crush and jostle themselves in
the mud and darkness, and because of fear of death, remain
among evils from failure to believe in the joy of the beyond.

The burst of "marvelous light" is the *dromena*, which Pound
suggested to me was an orgasm. Yet I think the spiritual significance of the ritual was more important to him. In the *Usura*
canto (45) he has the famous line, "They have brought whores
for Eleusis," meaning that the usurers have profaned a shrine.

Pound, who loved to revise history, even went so far as to
identify the tradition of Eleusis with the heresy of the Albigensians. No account of the troubadours would be complete without some mention of the Albigensian Crusade (1209–1249). The
term "Albigensian" is from the town of Albi in the Tarn, where
the huge cathedral looks more like a fortress than a church. In
that region a sect of heretics became prevalent which so troubled
Pope Innocent III that he had the Inquisition destroy them with
the greatest violence. These heretics were also called Cathars,
meaning "the pure ones" (from the Greek "katharos"). They
believed in the coexistence of two principles, good and evil, represented by God and the Devil. Light was opposed to dark, the
soul to the body, and this life to the next. Like the Gnostics, they
believed that Jesus was figurative, "an emanation from the First
Cause." That is, the Cathars considered that Jesus was sent by
God as an angel, and only appeared to have a physical pres-
ence. Thus the crucifixion, or any other human attributes, were,
for them, inconceivable. They were ascetic and pledged to absolute chastity. They were vegetarians. To get to Heaven sooner
some of them practiced suicide by starvation. A bad lot, obvi-
ously, and Rome eradicated them in the first crusade launched
against a Christian country.

But, as Pound discerned, much of the incentive for the
slaughter was political. It was a power struggle for control of the
South of France. Back of Simon de Montfort, the Pope's man,
was the King of France, who controlled the North and wanted
the South. Back of Count Raymond of Toulouse, who supported

the Albigensians, was the Spanish Peter II of Aragon. As Pound writes in Canto 74, "Les Albigeois, a problem of history." And in *The Spirit of Romance* he describes the Albigensian Crusade as "a sordid robbery cloaking itself in religious pretence [that] ended the *gai savoir* in southern France." Most historians agree that the persecution of the Cathars with the attendant destruction of so many feudal castles and the economy which supported them virtually ended the high culture of Provence and brought the art of the troubadours to its conclusion.

If Justin Smith's *The Troubadours at Home* was an early inspiration for Pound, a curious and obscure book, *Le Secret des Troubadours* by a French Rosicrucian who called himself "Sâr Péladan," which Pound read about 1906, may have directed him to the linkage between Eleusis and the Albigensians. Pound reviewed Péladan's book unfavorably at the time but the thesis seems to have stuck in his head.

Pioneering Interpretations

It is now seventy-seven years since Pound published his first versions of troubadour poetry in *The Spirit of Romance*. How are his translations standing up? Not an easy question to answer for one who admires him so much. Very well, I think, in one way, not so well in another. As pioneering interpretations—the Victorian translations have little feeling for the tone of the originals—they are superb. Pound was the first, at least in English, to understand what the troubadours were trying to do, and in what the metric of *motz el son* consisted. As such they are a landmark in cultural history.

The difficulty is that the poems are not easy to read. They require considerable concentration and patience. The reader today, because it is our present poetic idiom, is accustomed to free verse and, for the most part, natural, sometimes almost colloquial, voice cadences. But what Pound gave us is highly complex word machines. Take one of the finest canzos of Arnaut Daniel, the "Doutz brais e critz," which begins by imitating bird songs. Here we can note how different are the sounds of Provençal

words from those of Latin or the other Romance languages. So
many short, stabbing words with harsh endings. The first two of
seven stanzas:

> Doutz brais e critz,
> Lais e cantars e voutas
> Aug dels auzels qu' en lur latins fant precs
> Quecs ab sa par, atressi cum nos fam
> A las amigas en cui entendem;
> E doncas ieu qu' en la genssor entendi
> Dei far chansson sobre totz de bell' obra
> Que noi aia mot fals mi rima estrampa.

> Non fui marritz
> Ni non presi destoutas
> Al prim qu' intriei el chastel dinz los decs,
> Lai on estai midonz, don ai gran fam
> C' anc non l' ac tal lo nebotz Sain Guillem;
> Mil vetz lo jorn en badaill em n' estendi
> Per la bella que totas austras sobra
> Tant cant val mais fis gaugz qu' ira ni rampa.

And then Pound:

> Sweet cries and cracks
> and lays and chants inflected
> By auzels who, in their Latin belikes,
> Chirm each to each, even as you and I
> Pipe toward those girls on whom our thoughts attract;
> Are but more cause that I, whose overweening
> Search is toward the noblest, set in cluster
> Lines where no word pulls wry, no rhyme breaks gauges.

> No culs de sacs
> nor false ways me deflected
> When first I pierced her fort within its dykes,
> Hers for whom my hungry insistency

Passes the gnaw whereby was Vivien wracked;*
Day-long I stretch, all times, like a bird preening,
And yawn for her, who hath o'er others thrust her
As high as true joy is o'er ire and rages.

In the first line of each stanza Pound imitates the sharp sounds of Arnaut's rhyme words. "Critz/ marritz/ grazitz/ chauzitz, floritz/ ditz/ deschausitz" become "cracks/ sacs/ lax/ tax/ wax/ knacks/ jacks."

Pound was also attentive to line lengths, syllabic patterns, and visual appearance on the page. Arnaut's "L'aura amara" uses a line that is unusually short for troubadour verse. Perhaps it was related to the tempo of the music to which he was singing. We do not know what troubadour music was like. Some fragments of crude notation survive but musicologists interpret them differently. The notation shows position on the staff, but there are no indications for measure, duration or rhythm. The music appears to have been monodic. As for the instruments, there are no contemporary pictures. Based on the miniatures in anthologies made some centuries later, the French authority Jacques Roubaud believes that the jongleurs may have played on a psaltery, a "naquaire," a lute, a cymbal, a cromorne, a flute, or a vielle (hurdy-gurdy).[4] When we made the New York Center's documentary film on Pound, our Occitan performer sang Arnaut for us with a vielle in the courtyard of the castle at Excideuil, birthplace of the troubadour Giraut de Borneil. The vielle sounded rather like a syncopated bagpipe, not melodious.

The first of six stanzas and a coda of Arnaut's "L'aura amara":

L'aura amara
Fals bruoills brancutz
Clarzir
Quel doutz espeissa ab fuoills,
Els letz
Becs

---

* Vivien, an allusion to Sain Guillem.

Dels auzels ramencs
Ten balps e mutz,
Pars
E non-pars;
Per qu' eu m' esfortz
De far e dir
Plazers
A mains per liei
Que m' a virat bas d' aut,
Don tem morir
Sils afans no m' asoma.

And Pound:

The bitter air
Strips panoply
From trees
Where softer winds set leaves,
And glad
Beaks
Now in brakes are coy,
Scarce peep the wee
Mates
And un-mates
   What gaud's the work?
   What good the glees?
What curse
I strive to shake!
Me hath she cast from high,
In fell disease
I lie, and deathly fearing.

Pound's translations are incredibly agile feats of replication. He understood that the rhyme and syllabic structures were a functional element of the poems. He was determined to bring them across. Roubaud tells us that some 2600 troubadour texts have survived, almost all in copies from later than the twelfth century, and in them about nine hundred rhyme patterns may be found. Invention was important to the jongleurs. It was "make it new" on a small scale. If a man could not only write well and sing well but also invent variant stanzaic forms, that was to his credit.

Pound's concern for getting the rhymes into English led him into artificial diction. He had to turn to archaic words and to reversals of normal word order—something which went against his later poetic practice in his own work. The criteria for Imagism speak only of "composing in sequence of the musical phrase," but in the *ABC of Reading*, where he is setting "tests and composition exercizes" for students, he goes further, asking the pupils "how many words are out of their usual place, and whether this alteration makes the statement in any way more interesting or more energetic."

"Chirm" in his version of "Doutz brais e critz" is an example of his use of archaisms. The O.E.D. derives it from Anglo-Saxon and gives as its first meaning "to cry out or roar"; another meaning, "to chatter or warble, as birds." It is plain why Pound chose the word. The "ch" sound is akin to certain Provençal sounds. And it is *short*, as so many Provençal words are. "Warble" or "chatter" would have been too long, and too conventional.

Pound's love of archaic words probably began when he was a child. His mother Isabel, a cousin of Longfellow on the Wadsworth side, greatly desired that he become a poet. She pushed him to read and he read all his life. He had an astonishing memory. I don't think he ever forgot a word he had seen. We know from the *Cantos* what the past meant to him. Old words were a link with the past, with tradition. The early poems of the Venice period use many archaisms, but they drop away in the later sections of *Personae*. In the *Cantos* they are used mostly for historical color. The style of Pound's Provençal poems is no longer very palatable. The archaic words are stumbling blocks. The inversions of word order often make it hard to get the sense at a single reading. We have to puzzle it out. The lines do not flow. It adds up to a verbal tone that is a bit affected and even "poeticky."

It is a truism that each generation needs new translations of the classics. Such modern-idiom translators as Fitts and Fitzgerald, Arrowsmith and Nims, Emily Vermeule and David Grene have rescued the Greek plays from the sludge of Gilbert Murray. There will be new translators to carry on what Pound began with the troubadours, and there shoud be. Paul Blackburn's versions in *Proensa* (1978) signal what can be done. Blackburn came to the troubadours through Pound. He was a devotee of Pound's poetry. But he had learned the lesson of the rhyme schemes and boldly decided to sacrifice them. He based his cadences on those of his own original poems, working out what I would describe as a heightened and enriched colloquial style-tone. This passage is from Peire Vidal's "Ab l'alan tir vas me l'aire":

> But why keep me in such a confusion?
> She must know that nothing ever pleased me so much.
> From that first hour,
> the first touch,
> I could not split my heart, my love, my mind
> away from what I'd found. So
> that now if she harms me, it's bound to be
> a disaster for me.
> But if she gives me token
> of accord and friendship, then it's certain
> she couldn't offer greater grace or mercy
> And if she need a reason to be right,
> let it
> be that her love sustains me.

Blackburn could not have made such a fine English poem, could not have captured the feeling of Vidal so well, if Pound had not led the way. I think the master would be proud of his pupil.

RAMBLING AROUND
POUND'S *PROPERTIUS*

Propertius Comes to Harvard Yard

At Choate, in 1931, it was not H. P. ("Hup-Hup") Arnold, the classics master, but the poet Dudley Fitts who started me on Propertius. "Hup," who skipped the part about Dido and Aeneas in the cave in the *Aeneid*, knew that *Integer Vitae* built character in boys but that the Elegaic Poets would not sit with the Head, whose great sermon on the Honest Sailor who reported an errant master was repeated annually to a cheering audience in chapel.[1]

Sextus Propertius's name came up a few days after I enrolled at the Ezuversity in Rapallo in 1934 and was loaned a marked-up copy of the Mueller edition.[2] But I didn't get deep into what Pound had done with him until I was reading the Elegiac Poets at Harvard with Professor E. K. Rand. What a charming and learned man! And those were still the days when doctors made house calls and great professors invited students to dinner and served port.

Professor Rand was not a noddy like Professor William Hale, who reviewed Pound's *Homage to Sextus Propertius* as a *translation* in *Poetry* magazine. Rand's favorite work of modern poetry was Robert Bridges's *Testament of Beauty*.[3] But he was willing to talk about Eliot and Pound, unlike his colleague the Boylston Professor of Rhetoric, Robert Hillyer, who was known to eject students from his classroom for mentioning their names. So I

ventured to offer Rand a paper on Pound's *Propertius,* this about
1937. With him I had no worry that the visits to his study where
I could examine his classic texts printed by Aldus and Estienne
and Didot would cease. I defined the *Propertius* immediately as a
transcription, but hedged with some comments about "egregious
errors,": "sitiens"—"sitting," "vota"—"vote"—and the "dis-
tortions" of the collage structure. Then I let fly with praise of
Pound's "verbal valence" (we had our innocuous terminologies
in those days, too) in the *Nox mihi candida* (Night that is shining
for me) which Pound rendered: "Me, happy, night, night full of
brightness." Professor Rand was advised (as if he didn't know)
that in the *Propertius* he could watch "the metamorphosis of ob-
servation into imagination," that Pound favored "terminal syzy-
gies," but that (take care!) "Propertius seems to have been an
ill-disciplined person subject to rapid and violent changes of
mood." However I went too far when I suggested that the Emperor Augustus was Propertius's Sir Basil Zaharoff (Metevsky).[4]
The line was crossed out in red with no comment.

The comment at the end of my paper was: "A judicious evalu-
ation. But a little more care with your syntax, please." And below that a line from Propertius: "Cur tua praescripto sevecta est
pagina gyro?" (Why has your page swerved from the ring pre-
scribed for it?)

Those Welsh Mines

According to Donald Gallup, Pound's bibliographer, the *Propertius* first appeared in Pound's 1919 book *Quia Pauper Amavi,*
which also contained "Langue d'Oc," "Moeurs Contemporaines," and three Ur-Cantos. When Pound translated the Latin
phrase (from Ovid) for me as "Love on the dole," I saw to what
the title applied. Propertius was well-to do but he lost his family
estates when they were given to veterans, and he wrote "Ergo
sollicitate tu causa pecunia vitae." (So, money, you it is that are
the cause of worry in life.) In their London days the Pounds
were living on Ezra's small literary jobs, Dorothy's allowance,
and an occasional ten dollar bill (which bought a lot then) in

Homer's letters from Wyncote. Can not their situation support the thesis that Pound made *his* Propertius more anti-establishment than Propertius really was because of his own growing dislike of the banking system? "The bank makes it *ex nihil*," Pound writes in Canto 46. Sullivan records that the *Propertius* was completed in 1918. Pound did not meet Major Douglas in the office of the *New Age* until 1918, but he had been researching the causes of war since shortly after Gaudier's death.

I suspect that the "Welsh mines" passage may prove my point. "Cimbrorumque minas et benefacta Mari" means, more or less: "the threat of Cimbrian invasion (wild men from Wales pillaging the Roman settlements in Britain) and Marus's public service and the profit in defeating them." But Pound makes it " . . . Welsh mines and the profit Marus had out of them." *Minas* cannot mean mines. No way. Mines would be *metalla*. But the line rang a bell with Ezra and he saw how he could use it to get at his enemies, the bankers and their military stooges. This sort of thing goes on constantly in the *Propertius*—it is part of the mask mechanism—but it is seldom so clear-cut. Usually it is done for irony or humor, which gives the poem its marvelous flavor.

In our correspondence Ezra teased me a good deal, usually referring to my "Haavud iggurance," and I sometimes teased him back. I wrote him in 1935 that those mines were really a bit too much, and received this reply:

> The Homage is on a list of mine somewhere as a persona [which means he was writing under the guise or mask of another person]. D/n suppose S propertius hadn'd died/ or had RipvanWinkled, and come to and wrote a poem/ In yanqui. I NEVER said the Homage was a translation. Some of it coincides/ as if I rewrote a poem I had done twenty years ago/ The Hardy [Thomas Hardy] prob/ Hit it when he said it wd/ have helped the boob reader if I had called it "S. P. soliloquizes." "boob"/ is not textual. Mr. Hardy's langwidg waz choicer. Continuin'/ My contribution to classical scholarship if any/ wd. consist in blasting the idea that Propertius wd. have been an editor of the New Republic/ or that

he was a moon-headed decorator/ smaragdos chrysolithosve, As
thesis it wd be that he had a bean/ plus a bit of humor and irony
which the dessicated do not see . . . Perhaps 'nowhere seeking to
make or to avoid translation' wd. answer query.

On the Palatine Hill

Atra dies. One of my blackest days. All during the shooting of
Lawrence Pitkethly's documentary on Pound in 1981 (as an old
friend of Ezra's I was supposed to be the continuity figure, but
the film editor left most of my continuations on the cutting room
floor) as we traipsed in a van from troubadour country, through
the Sacred Places and finally to Rome, I was dreaming of my
Great Event. I had been promised that I could do the *Nox mihi
candida*, one of the greatest love poems of all time, on the Pala-
tine Hill. The day came. I had rented a toga in the Via della
Scrofula. The shooting went on. I waited. The light was fading.
Lawrence was making more and more useless shots of memorial
arches. (I think he is queer for arches.) "Lawrence," I pleaded,
"you promised." The cameraman took a light reading and said,
"It's too late for that now." "You can at least do it on tape,"
Lawrence said. I gave a magnificent declamation. And only then
noticed that the tape was not running. I wasn't even worth a bit
of tape. The film will be on PBS in 1988, but I don't care if you
watch it. I was betrayed.

Die Stimme hinter dem Vorhang

I have a great admiration for Donald Davie. With R. P. Blackmur
and John Espey, he was one of the first critics to make high
claims for Pound. In our present climate that sounds simple
enough; but Espey told me the story of how his professors,
when he announced that he would do his dissertation on
Pound, begged him not to destroy his academic career before it
had even begun.

My admiration for Davie recently increased when I heard him

do a superb hatchet job, so elegant and so witty, on some neo-Marxists and post-structuralists whom Terry Terrell had imported to the Pound Conference at Orono, Maine, in 1985. I felt, as Davie punctured those gaseous balloons of non-signification, that he was speaking for Ez, who was muttering "Cat-piss and porcupines!" It was a bravura performance. Davie is also a fine poet; the master always told me that good poets were the ones qualified to explain poetry.

But there have been moments when D. D. puzzled me. First at Noel Stock's Pound conference at Toledo, Ohio in 1971 when he remarked that D. H. Lawrence and Williams — two of my heroes — were a pernicious influence on his writer-students.[5] And I was puzzled when I read in his book on Pound that the *Propertius* was composed in "Babu English," or "translatorese." I had spent some time working in India, doing cultural Boy Scout jobs for the Ford Foundation in 1954. This meant hours sitting in the offices of minor functionaries of the Ministry of Education, tedious hours while the punkahs whined and barefoot but turbaned peons were sent scurrying after file folders. I had those bureaucratic intonations pretty well fixed in my head; they were indeed curious, but I could not relate them to what I heard in the *Propertius*. There was a correspondence of idiom in the more political passages, where, as Hugh Kenner points out, Pound is using the "Latinate polysyllables" to deride the Establishment, but that seemed to me a matter of vocabulary, not of poetic cadence. Who or what was it that I was hearing? Was it only Pound's lines of prose in the *Cantos*?

I put the problem on hold. And it wasn't until 1983 when we went to Hexham in Northumbria to interview that grand old man Basil Bunting (R.I.P.) for Pitkethly's documentary that I found what seemed a satisfactory answer. That was for me an historic day. We had set up the lights and the camera in the living room of the cottage. "The Bas" sparkled his eyes at us and talked away, as only he could talk, while he nipped at the Scotch we had brought him.

He told some remarkable stories about his life in Persia, as a seaman on the Murmansk run and in the RAF in Italy, good tales about Pound, but most of the talk was on poetry, particularly melopoeia. He told us that when Pound came to London in 1908 "he was forty years behind" and that "his father—and his mother—were Rossetti." But Pound knew that Yeats was "the great living poet to go after." Some ten years later Yeats would tell Bunting that Pound had devised the best *vers libre* structure yet done in English. It was, Bunting said, "in the *Homage* that Pound discovered how to organize a poem on the model of music so that every line grows out of the line before by modification. The effect is very much like the sonata form." "Was there," I asked, "a basic rhythm?" There was indeed, he assured me, and it was—Whitman. I was amazed. I can't recall that Pound ever talked about Whitman at the Ezuversity sessions, though his poem beginning "I make a pact with you, Walt Whitman . . ." is well known and there is the little known two-page essay "What I feel about Walt Whitman" (1955) buried in the *Selected Prose* collection. But I had never made a metrical connection, although Pound writes in the essay: "As for Whitman, I read him (in many parts) with acute pain, but when I write of certain things I find myself using his rhythms." Bunting went on to recite the beginning of "Out of the cradle endlessly rocking," beating time with his finger; then he did part of Pound's translation of the "Nox mihi candida." The echo was clear to all of us.

> Fool who would set a term to love's madness,
> For the sun shall drive with black horses,
> earth shall bring wheat from barley,
> The flood shall move toward the fountain
> Ere love know moderations,
> The fish shall swim in dry streams.
> No, now while it may be, let not the fruit of life cease.

What clinched the argument for me was Bunting telling us that once, years before, he had gotten stuck reciting the Whitman poem to Ezra; then Ezra had picked up and carried through to the end without a pause. The poem was permanently in his head.

That was a great day in Hexham. We had lunch in the village pub, then continued shooting. At about three the bottle of Scotch was empty; "The Bas's" chin declined to his chest and he slipped softly into slumber. We had had a course in the bond between poetry and music, and what Pound had made with it. Only a fraction of the interview found its way into the film, but the out-takes are safe and I hope that a video cassette will be edited from them.

The Sounds of the Old Words

I ask whether some of the beaneries may be paddling the young up shit creek? Is poking a computer as conducive to the formation of style as reading Plato or Virgil? (And by style I don't mean this parody of E.P. talking at the lunch table of the Ezuversity. I mean the way Leon Edel or Harry Levin writes prose.) I submit that style is heard in the head as it is put down, and that those sounds come from reading the right texts in youth: the classics in the originals, the King James Version of the Bible, even the Gettysburg Address.

When I was invited to do Pound and Williams at Brown I warned the students that I would not turn in their grades until I had heard them recite four lines of Latin. (My wife said this reminded her of Radcliffe when the girls had to swim across the pool in order to graduate.) I let the students choose anything that pleased them, even Catullus 80 if they liked that sort of thing. I simply wanted them to have in their heads the sound of some good Latin words and how the words move in the line, "rubbing themselves" on each other forwards and backwards.

Since we were doing the *Propertius*, most chose from him, and the favorite turned out to be the "dum nos fata sinunt," lines that echo in my own head though I suppose they are sentimental.

> dum nos fata sinunt, oculos satiemus amore
> nox tibi longa venit, nec reditura dies
> (While our fates twine together, sate we our eyes with love;
> For long night comes upon you and a day when no day returns.)

Not long afterward I was "Loebing" my way through Tibullus and was startled to come on exactly the same line.[6] I even found one in Catullus that isn't far from it. What does this tell us about the literary life in Rome? Were the boys cribbing from each other? Or paying compliments by imitation? Or was this a poetic convention of the time? John Speirs points out that many scholars believe that much of Propertius was drawn from Callimachus—hard to prove since so little of Callimachus survives. And would it have been Kenner who remarked that what the Elegiac Poets *say* is not extremely profound; what they do with the words gives their poetry its charge.

A Backward Glance

Not everyone has seen Pound's 1911 (*Canzoni*) translation of Propertius, III, 26, because it was dropped from *Personae*, though it is now in the *Collected Early Poems*. It bears looking at to see how much Pound improved in eight years.

PRAYER FOR HIS LADY'S LIFE (1911)

From Propertius, *Elegiae*, Lib. III, 26

Here let thy clemency, Persephone, hold firm,
Do thou, Pluto, bring here no greater harshness.
So many thousand beauties are gone down to Avernus
Ye might let one remain above with us.

With you is Iope, with you the white-gleaming Tyro,
With you is Europa and the shameless Pasiphae,
And all the fair from Troy and all from Achaia,
From the sundered realms, of Thebes and of aged Priamus;
And all the maidens of Rome, as many as they were,
They died and the greed of your flame consumes them.

Here let thy clemency, Persephone, hold firm,
Do thou, Pluto, bring here no greater harshness.

So many thousand fair are gone down to Avernus,
Ye might let one remain above with us.

Then the abridged version in *Homage to Sextus Propertius*, ix, 2 (1919):

Persephone and Dis, Dis, have mercy upon her,
There are enough women in hell,
          quite enough beautiful women,
Iope, and Tyro, and Pasiphae, and the formal girls of Achaia,

And out of Troad, and from the Campania,
Death has his tooth in the lot,
          Avernus lusts for the lot of them,
Beauty is not eternal, no man has perennial fortune,
Slow foot, or swift foot, death delays but for a season.

See what has happened. Some of the mythological fustian has been cut, to advantage, but the great change is this: the tame and trite "So many thousand beauties are gone down to Avernus" has become the superb "There are enough women in hell, quite enough beautiful women" for "sunt apud infernos tot milia formasarum." It's like going from Sully Prudhomme to Laforgue.

*   *   *

Nuggets

T. S. Eliot (1919)

The *Homage* is a new *persona*, a creation of a new character, recreating Propertius in himself, and himself in Propertius.

Professor W. G. Hale (1919)

Mr Pound is incredibly ignorant of Latin. He has of course a perfect right to be, but not if he translates from it. The result of his ignorance is that much of what he makes his author say is unintelligible. . . . If Mr Pound were a professor of Latin, there would be nothing left for him but suicide.

E.P. (in a letter to Orage, 1919)

Hale pretends to read Latin, but has apparently never *understood* anything but syntax and never seen the irony of Propertius . . . Re decadence: We all know that Propertius went to mid-week prayer meeting. . . . If I were, however, a professor of Latin in Chicago, I should probably have to resign on divulging the fact that Propertius occasionally copulavit, i.e. rogered the lady to whom he was not legally wedded.

Robert Nichols (1920)

In place of the quiet and tender irony we are accustomed to see upon the face of Thomas Campion's favourite Latin poet we behold a mask of gaiety and elegiac irony, sometimes almost saturnine . . . the voice is not that of the professional gramophone, being at least a live voice. That is, however, I fear, all that can be said for the version. . . . Mr Pound is not, never has been and almost, I might hazard, never will be, a poet. He is too hard, too clever; he has yet to learn that poetry does not so much glitter as shine.

Wyndham Lewis (in reply to the Nichols review, 1920)

Mr Pound, without being a pedant, may conceivably know that Chaucer, Landor, Ben Jonson, and many contemporaries of Rowlandson, found other uses for classic texts than that of making literal English versions of them. Or, again, that the parody of Yeats . . . and the mention of Wordsworth . . . would have indicated to a sensitive or less biassed critic that Mr Pound... had some other aim than that of providing a crib for schoolboys or undergraduates.

Ford Madox Ford (1926)

What is the *Homage* but a prolonged satire upon our own day, as if Propertius should come to New York or London...

R. P. Blackmur (1933)

What is characteristic of this poem more than its attitudes toward love and toward the poet's profession, is the elegance of the language in which these attitudes are expressed. By elegance is meant... a consistent choice of words and their arrangement such as to exemplify a single taste...

... the element of conversational, colloquial ease used formally, almost rhetorically to heighten the seriousness of the verse.

Hugh Kenner (1951)

By 1917 Pound had forged a new language; not only the expression, but the sensibility brought to the Latin, is liberated from Victorian emotional cliché.... a block of speech and perception new to the English poetic tradition, and a use of language that responds to the pressures of perception with (Ching Ming) accuracy and adequacy.

Pound... brought to Propertius' Elegies a sensibility alert to elegant cynicism, informed by Laforgue's dealings with pretentious sentiment and pretentious bombast alike.

The deliberate *collage* of poker-faced misreadings performed by Pound in certain portions of this poem should perhaps be connected with the exploration of these zones of consciousness initiated by Joyce five years later.

.... the enormous freedom and range of tone, the ironic weight, the multiple levels of tongue-in-cheek self-deprecation everywhere present in the *Propertius*.

(1971)

The *Homage*... was achieved by a mind filled with James's prose ... Not only the ghost of the Latin elegiac couplet presides over its way of dividing discourse, but the great ghost also, "phantom" with weighted motion, that drank (he wrote thenabouts) "the tone of things," and spaced its discourse with suspenseful deliberateness.

(1983, from an interview transcript from the documentary made by Pitkethly)

JL : Why was Pound attracted to Propertius?
HK : A lot of things came together... the fascination with the poet whom the establishment has missed ... the wars and rumors of wars in Rome which rhymes with the British imperial propaganda of 1917... and then finally there was the opportunity presented by the enormous number of Latin words embedded in the English language that he could use in the poem ... from which he got a strange tone of abstract superciliousness... just what he wanted.

* * *

The Tradition

1. Sir Charles Elton (1778–1835) Propertius II, 3

> 'Twas not her face, though fair, that caught my sight;
> Less fair the lily's bell: as Scythian snows
> Should blend with Ebro's red their virgin white,
> Or in pure cream as floats the scatter'd rose:

Not tresses, that enring'd in crisped twine,
    Flow loose with their accustom'd careless art
Down her smooth marble neck; nor eyes that shine,
    Torches of passion; lode-stars of my heart:

Not that through silken folds of Araby
    The nymph's fine limbs with lucid motion gleam;
(For no ideal beauties heaves my sigh;
    Nor airy nothings prompt my amorous dream:)

2. From Kathy Acker: *Blood and Guts in High School* (New York: Grove Press, 1986).

Propertius is staring blankly at the door and scratching his head.

Cynthia : DON'T FUCK ME 'CAUSE YOU LIKE THE SMELL OF MY CUNT, LEAVE ME ALONE. This is the only way I can directly speak to you cause you're autistic.
Propertius : This is my poem to your cunt door.

    Oh little door
    I love you so very much.

Cynthia : Well, everyone wants to fuck me I tell you I'm sick of this life. Who cares if you're another person waiting at my door? You're just another man and you don't mean shit to me.
Propertius : Oh please, cunt, I'm cold and I'll be the best man for you and I know you're fucking someone else that's why you won't let me near you you cheap rags stinking fish who wants anything to do with corpses anyway? (*to himself*) And thus I tried to drown my mourning.

3. Auctor Ignotus, 1983

NO MY DEAR

I'll not wish you the death
you deserve sunt apud infer-

nos tot milia formasarum
there are enough women in

hell quite enough beauti-
ful women but it is not

sufficient my dear to be
as beautiful as you are

despicit et magnos recte
puella deos and of all

these young women not one
has enquired the cause of

the world so go your way
my dear and I'll go mine.

AN INTRODUCTION
TO THE *CANTOS*

As we commemorate the hundredth anniversary
of Ezra Pound's birth (October 30, 1985) we think immediately
of his *Cantos*, written between 1919 and 1961 — 117 of them in
nearly eight hundred pages.[1] Technically they are his most inno-
vative writing and in content they are the most extraordinary.
The short poems of Pound's *Personae* collection will probably
always be his most popular work because they are accessible.
His English versions of Chinese, Japanese, Greek, Latin, and
Provençal poetry and plays are among the finest translations
made in this century. And his literary essays and such books of
criticism as the *ABC of Reading, Guide to Kulchur*, and *The Spirit of
Romance* are as provocative as they are iconoclastic. But Pound
intended the *Cantos* to be his testament, and many consider
them his masterpiece.

From Aural Memory

All the *Cantos* were written out of a prodigious memory, and
especially the finest section, *The Pisan Cantos*, done when Pound
was incarcerated in the Army's Disciplinary Training Center
near Pisa following his repulsive Rome broadcasts made during
the war. The myriad details of persons, places, history, and various literatures all came from memory. And so it was throughout
the composition of the long poem, except when he was working
from a particular source such as a Renaissance manuscript, or de

Mailla's *Histoire générale de la Chine*, or such correspondence as that of John Adams and Thomas Jefferson.

Pound's memory was more aural than visual. His incredible ear picked up the sounds of words in any language. The number of "original" spellings, particularly of proper names, in the *Cantos* might bear out that theory. When he was in the heat of composing a canto he didn't want to stop to do much checking. And reading proofs bored him. Consistency also bored him; he would often make different corrections in his English and American proofs. This presented problems for his editors because his allusions were not often to be found in the usual reference books. Once in the 1960s when I was visiting him in Rapallo and was badgering him about some spellings that didn't look right, he closed the book very firmly and said, "Why don't you abolish the *Cantos*?"

Models and Sources

Pound's models for the *Cantos* were primarily the epics of Homer and Dante. How he transformed those models, driven as he was to write a new kind of *personal* epic, is one of the wonders and enigmas of modern literature. Pound's poetic idiom seldom sounds "modern." We can still hear in the *Cantos* overtones of Campion and Waller, Rossetti and Browning, even Whitman. Where he broke with the past, where he became modern, was in the arrangement of the lines, in his experiments with a collage structure. This making of collages and his practice of weaving into the text words and whole passages from some thirteen languages, ancient and modern, including even Chinese characters, perplex many readers.

One of Pound's premises as he began writing the *Cantos* was that an epic was a poem "containing history." But he enlarged his scope as the poem progressed. New ingredients were added, such as the monetary reform theories of C. H. Douglas (Social Credit) and Silvio Gesell. And early on, in Canto 13, Pound added to his master plan the ethics of Confucius. We find ten cantos of early Chinese history (52–61) drawn from the

chronicles of the French Jesuit Joseph-Anne-Marie Moyriac de
Mailla, which show how China prospered when a good emperor
followed Confucian principles and what happened to the people
when a bad emperor did not. Confucianism tied in with economics—a "Confucian" emperor would have a clean economic
system.

The Confucian ethic was not the only gift from Chinese culture to the *Cantos*. Quite as important was Pound's "ideogrammatic method" for structuring the poem. This technique came
partly to Pound from his study of classic Chinese poetry as seen
in his little book *Cathay*, which he published in 1915, working
from the notes of the scholar Ernest Fenollosa. Here is the beginning of "Poem by the Bridge at Ten-Shin":

> March has come to the bridge head,
> Peach boughs and apricot boughs hang over a thousand gates
> At morning there are flowers to cut the heart,
> And evening drives them on the eastward-flowing waters.

This is straightforward English, but if we look at Fenollosa's
notebooks (a crib of early Chinese poetry that emphasized all
the nouns and verbs in the verses), now in the Beinecke Library
at Yale, we see what Pound saw, that there are few syntactical
connecting words between those that carry the meanings.
Image rubs against image. Years later, we find Pound applying
this principle in the *Cantos*. Words, phrases, whole sentences
become "ideograms" that are placed together without the usual
connectives. These disjuncts, treated like collage in painting,
work on one another to show relationships that enlarge the total
meaning of a passage. In *Canto* 110 we find a theme from Greek
mythology juxtaposed with one from Japanese Buddhism:

> And in thy mind beauty, O Artemis,
>> as of mountain lakes in the dawn,
> Foam and silk are thy fingers
>>> Kuanon,

and the long suavity of her moving,
     willow and olive reflected.

Can we enjoy only what Pound jokingly called the "beauty spots" of the *Cantos*, the simple parts where there are extended passages of sequential narrative or description? Are the rapid collages and the recondite allusions too much for us? Pound seems to assume his reader knows everything and everyone he does. He provided no notes for the *Cantos*. If we want to know who Gollievski or "old Jarge" were, we must go to Carroll F. Terrell's *Companion to the Cantos of Ezra Pound*. But how much does it really matter who they were if the lines in which they appear are interesting? Did the readers of Dante know who all those people in the *Commedia* were?

Quoting the fifteenth-century Dutch scholar Rudolphus Agricola, Pound defines the purpose of literature in Canto 89 as "Ut moveat, ut doceat, ut dilectet."[2] Literature should move us, teach us, and delight us. Do the *Cantos* meet this test? "Ut moveat"—some of us are moved by the fate that the gods, or history, impose on us; it's all there in the *Cantos*. "Ut doceat"—except for the sciences, a rich college curriculum awaits us in the poem. "Ut dilectet"—there is no finer music or language in the work of any poet of our time:

> And then went down to the ship,
> Sat keel to breakers, forth on the godly sea, and
> We set up mast and sail on that swart ship,
> Bore sheep aboard her, and our bodies also
> Heavy with weeping, and winds from sternward
> Bore us out onward with bellying canvas.
>
> —CANTO 1

> With the first pale-clear of the heaven
> And the cities set in their hills,
> And the goddess of the fair knees
> Moving there, with the oak-woods behind her,

The green slope, with white hounds
    leaping about her.

                   — CANTO 17

What thou lovest well remains,
                  the rest is dross
What thou lov'st well shall not be reft from thee
What thou lov'st well is thy true heritage
Whose world, or mine or theirs
                 or is it of none?
First came the seen, then thus the palpable
  Elysium, though it were in the halls of hell,
What thou lovest well is thy true heritage.

                   — CANTO 81

Structure

Pound liked to be mysterious about his work and the references in it. He was not the kind of author who calls up (usually collect) in the middle of the night to tell what is going to be in the next chapter. Once I asked Olga Rudge if he explained his work to her. She said that he never talked about his work, he just wrote it. What Ezra would usually answer if his father asked him what he was writing was simply "wait and see," but in one letter to Homer Pound he is more communicative:

> Dear Dad, afraid the whole damn poem is rather obscure, especially in fragments. Have I ever given you outline of main scheme, or whatever it is. Rather like, or unlike subject and response and counter-subject in fugue. Live man goes down into world of dead. The repeat in history. The magic moment or moment of metamorphosis bust through from quotidian into divine or permanent world. Gods etc. Various things keep cropping up in the poem. The original world of gods, the Trojan War, Helen on the Wall of Troy, with the old men fed up with the whole show and suggesting she be sent back to Greece.

In the mid 1950s, when I was in Washington visiting Ezra at St. Elizabeths Hospital, I got him to talk briefly about the structure of the *Cantos*. When one went to visit him it was usually hard to get him to keep on the track because he was what they called "distracted." His mind would jump sideways, from subject to subject. But on this day he was very calm and he dictated notes on the *Cantos* to me.

  A. Dominated by the emotions.
  B. Constructive effort — Chinese Emperors and Adams, Putting order into things.
  C. Domination of benevolence. Theme in Canto 90. Cf. the thrones of Dante's "Paradiso."
  There will be 100 or 120 cantos, but it looks like 112.
  First 50 cantos are a detective story. Looking around to see what is wrong.
  Cantares — the Tale of the Tribe. To give the truth of history. Where Dante mentions a name, EP tries to give the gist of what the man was doing.

Then there is an interjection in my notes that I can't quite relate to the rest, but it's very nice:

  Cookie pushers who regard poetry as a bun shop and are busy making éclairs.

He talked next about the frescoes of del Cossa in the Palazzo Schifanoia, which means "chase away care," in Ferrara, which Pound saw after World War I:

  Schifanoia frescoes in three levels.
  Top. Allegories of the Virtues. (Cf. Petrarch's "Trionfi") study in values
  Middle. Signs of the Zodiac. Turning of the stars. Cosmology.
  Bottom. Particulars of life in the time of Borso d'Este.
  The contemporary

a) What is there—permanent—the sea
b) What is recurrent—the voyages
c) What is trivial—the casual—Vasco's troops weary, stupid parts.

That was the closest I ever came to getting him to outline the architecture of the *Cantos*, but I think that he changed his plans a great deal over the years as the poem lengthened.

A Long Monologue

If we stand back and look at the *Cantos* from a distance and ask, "What is really going on here?" we find that we are listening to a long monologue. Gertrude Stein said Pound was "a village explainer, excellent if you are a village, but if you are not, not." As night wears on in the village square the voice of the *Cantos* is explaining everything except science and technology.

In the early cantos the telling is very lively. Pound is full of excitement about his intellectual and esthetic discoveries—what he learned about the heroes and gods of the Mediterranean world; about Sigismondo Malatesta of Rimini, one of the most colorful of the warrior-princes of the Italian Renaissance; about Confucius; about the Chinese emperors (he liked best Emperor Tching Tang, who had engraved on his bathtub, "Make it new ... day by day make it new," which became Pound's motto, the goal for his own work); about the American founding fathers, particularly Jefferson and Adams. Pound weaves these disparate lives together with ingenuity. Their stories comment on one another; the process becomes a kind of moral criticism.

Later the mood of the *Cantos* changes, as Pound's situation has altered for the worse. The broadcasts he made from Rome during the war have brought him to the stockade. In *The Pisan Cantos* Pound is reflective and nostalgic, less didactic and more humble:

Pull down thy vanity
Thou art a beaten dog beneath the hail...

Pound, Rapallo, 1963.

> Pull down thy vanity
> I say pull down.
>
> When the mind swings by a grass-blade
> an ant's forefoot shall save you.

It is in *The Pisan Cantos* that we can approach Pound most closely as a person. He has had his turn of fortune and he is fearful for his future, but he isn't giving up. Birds perched on telephone wires remind him of notes of music. He enjoys the humor of the prisoners and guards. The gods of Greece are with him in his dark hour. And the goddess Aphrodite in Canto 79:

> This Goddess was born of sea-foam
> She is lighter than air under Hesperus
> δεινὰ εἶ, Κύθηρα
> terrible in resistance
> Κόρη καὶ Δήλια καὶ Μαῖα
> trine as praeludio
> Κύπρις Ἀφρόδιτη
> a petal lighter than sea-foam

Pound, Rapallo, 1963.

And he calls one of the Carrara mountains he sees from the camp "Taishan," which is a sacred mountain in China. The troubadours whom he had translated are with him. He recalls his good days as a young man in London. In some, though not all, of the three last segments of the *Cantos* the voice changes its tone again. It becomes more subdued, more meditative and speculative in Canto 116:

> But the beauty is not the madness
> Tho' my errors and wrecks lie about me.
> And I am not a demigod,
> I cannot make it cohere.
> If love be not in the house there is nothing.

In the later cantos Pound is looking back on his life. He is trying to put the pieces together. Dante had always been his model—hence the name "Cantos." If the early cantos are his "Inferno" and the middle ones his "Purgatorio," the "Section: Rock-Drill" ("I've got to drill it into their beans," he once told me) and "Thrones" (the third order of the angelic hierarchy in Dante) are his "Paradiso," his ascent to the higher realms of thought and the spirit.

The late cantos are the most difficult to grasp. Readers whom they baffle call them incoherent muttering. The ordering of lines is based on association from memory. These cantos are at first annoying—till we get the hang of them. But if we think of them as music they become clearer. Are they not fugal? There is a hidden structure. There are variations and recapitulations. The major themes in the earlier cantos are repeated and restated. Fragments are inserted in new combinations that give them deeper meaning. And the music of the language keeps pace with the subtlety of form.

The major motifs have now reached their full development. There is love, *Amor*, in its various aspects, as Pound had found it in the Eleusinian Mysteries of ancient Greece and in the love songs of the troubadours. There is nature as it appears in the myth of Demeter and Persephone. There is the ordering of the state as in Confucius and the good Chinese emperors, and in Duke Leopold of Siena and the founding fathers. Pound was not a professed Christian but there is religion or perhaps his own form of mysticism, seen in "the great ball of crystal—the acorn of light." This concept is rooted in his understanding of the nature of light, which is both Helios, the sun, and the light that shines in love. And above all there is the dream of the earthly paradise, the *"paradiso terrestre,"* which acceptance of his theories of economic reform might have made possible. (This paradise is figured in his mythical cities of Dioce and Wagadu.) These themes recur, sounding and seen together, for the *Cantos* are intensely visual. Everything is concrete and *shown*; there is very little symbolism and no extraneous rhetoric.

Pound and Williams

Toward the end of his life Pound worried about the *Cantos*. Had he managed to make them cohere? That is the salient question each reader must answer for himself. Certainly the *Cantos* do not cohere in the way *Paradise Lost* does. They are not tidy. But poetry moves in new ways; that is what insures its vitality from age to age. And if we look at the other personal epics of our century — Eliot's *Waste Land* and *Four Quartets*, Williams's *Paterson*, *The Bridge* by Hart Crane, Charles Olson's *Maximus Poems*, Louis Zukofsky's *"A"*, and Thomas Merton's *Geography of Lograire* — I think we can say that the *Cantos* do cohere, at least in the frame of modern poetry. In fact, the *Cantos* were the model, in whole or in part, for some of these other great poems. Olson acknowledged his debt to the *Cantos*. Williams never did, so far as I know, with respect to *Paterson*, but he knew the *Cantos* well and admired it, no matter how he felt about some of Pound's social attitudes. In a letter of 1940 Williams wrote me:

> It all revealed itself to me yesterday when I was reading his new Cantos, "Chinese Numbers" I calls it. He doesn't know a damn thing about China, the Chinese, or the language. That's what makes him an expert. He knows nothing about music, being tone deaf. That's what makes him a musician. He's a misplaced romantic. That's what makes him a historical realist. And he's batty in the head. That's what makes him a philosopher. But, in spite of it all, he's a good poet. I had to acknowledge it as I read along in that Chinese abacus frame of his enumerating verse. It had charm, it had sweep, it had even childish innocence written all over it. He thinks he's being terribly profound, frowningly serious, and all he's doing is building blocks, and it's lovely. He hasn't the least idea of where he hits true and where he falls flat. He wants to be praised for one thing, and he contradicts himself upon the same count in the next paragraph. He's got to be loved, to be praised, as one loves a mongoloid idiot; for his sweet character.

And in the same week—Pound was so much on Williams's mind—Bill wrote again about him:

It's easy to forget, in our dislike for some of the parts Ezra plays, and for which there is no excuse, that virtue can still be a mark of greatness.

It is hard to appraise, for the honors earned. It is even possible that Pound himself is self deceived and performs his miracles unconsciously while he frowns over some asininity he proposes and leans on so heavily. His language represents his last naiveté, the childishness of complete sincerity discovered in the child and the true poet alike. All that is necessary to feel Pound's excellence in this use of language, is to read the work of others, from whom I particularly and prominently exclude e. e. cummings. In the use of language, Pound and Cummings are beyond doubt, the two most distinguished American poets of today. It is the bringing over of the language of the day to the serious purposes of the poet, that is the difficult thing. Both of these men have evolved that ability to a high degree. Two faulty alternatives are escaped in the achievement of this distinction: there are plenty, who use the language well, fully as well as Pound, but for the trivial purposes either in journalism, fiction, or even verse. I mean the usual stroking of the meter without penetration, where anything of momentous significance is instinctively avoided; there are, on the other hand, poets of considerable seriousness, who simply do not know what language is and unconsciously load their compositions with the minute anachronisms, as many as dead hairs on a mangy dog. These, by virtue of all academic teaching, simply make their work no good. They would, and need to go through, the crises both Pound and Cummings experienced in ridding themselves of all collegiate taint. Not very nice to the "beaneries," as he used to call them. It is impossible to praise Pound's lines. The terms for such praise are lacking. There ain't none. You've got to read the line and feel first, then grasp through experience in its full significance, how the language makes the verse live. It lives. Even such uncompromising cataloguing as his Chinese kings, princes and other rulers, do live and become affecting under his treatment. It is the language, and the language only, that makes this true.

Yes, it is Pound's language that makes the *Cantos* an affecting work of literature. One of the cardinal terms in Williams's critical vocabulary was "the redeeming language." It is a major theme of *Paterson* and turns up in many of his essays. By it he meant not simply a language beautiful for poetry but also a language that might have an impact on society. The two poets sought their languages in very different ways: Williams, for the most part, in contemporary colloquial American speech; Pound in the speech of many cultures in many periods of history. Each, I think, found the redeeming language that was right for him.

SOME VOICES
FROM CANTO 74

Foreword

This piece began as a lecture, intended to illustrate and give voice
to the nine languages that were in Pound's head when he was
interned at the Disciplinary Training Center near Pisa in 1945 and
had to write *The Pisan Cantos* from memory with no books. I thought
of it first as a florilegium or oratorio. But as I worked on it, it came
to me that it might also be the scenario for a classroom performance,
with students reciting examples from the different languages.

As pedagogy, I think it works as a way for students to get the
sounds of the languages into their heads, just as Pound had done.
The students' first reactions were not favorable. "I've never
studied Greek." "I don't know Chinese." But if the parts are
short, it's amazing what can be done with phonetic memoriza-
tion. (Or students could be borrowed from other departments.)
The commentary, which should be drastically cut, might be re-
cited by the paidagogus (instructor) or different students, and the
prologue, a poem I wrote quoting from the *Cantos*, by a poet from
the class. There are recordings of the music of Pound's Cavalcanti
and Villon operas. For breaks between sections there are recordings of Pound's favorite English composers, Lawes and Jenkyns.

The organization of the selections which relate to Pound's references in Canto 74 was purely paratactic, or, we say now, by
"random selection." This in itself is a parody of Pound's famous
ideogrammatic method, in which elements not logically connected

are juxtaposed to illuminate each other by contrast and comparison. This is the basic structure of many parts of the *Cantos*. It
relates to the principle of collage in modern painting. Hugh Kenner often employs this type of structuring in his great historical-
critical work *The Pound Era*.

*   *   *

Some Voices from Canto 74

for V.J.

We know the scene;
The scene is a flat field north of Pisa
Where a small road runs west down to the sea
A flat field under Carrara   snow on the marble   "snow-white against
      stone-white on the mountain"
"In the death cells in sight of Mount Taishan" "one day were clouds
      banked on Taishan"
In a cage   in a tent   "If the hoar frost grip thy tent
                  Thou wilt give thanks when night is spent"
But the scene is really memory
In qual parte dove sta memoria   in that place where memory liveth
On the steps of the dogana   In the tempio at Rimini   by the
      belltower of San Pantaleone
Beside the Serpentine in London   "my London, your London"

      Ego scriptor   but who is the writer?   who is the speaker?
Perhaps the speaker is OU TIS   the speaker is No Man
He is "a man on whom the sun has gone down"
"A man of no fortune with a name to come"
Quis loquitur?   Are there many speakers?   Many voices?
Guido and Cino and il maestro di loro che sanno   the master of those
      who understood the truth
Arnaut and Bertran and François and old Peire Vidal
A little girl in China who longs for her husband's return
The chanters of the Noh

Kung in the Cedar grove   and Emperor Tching Tang making it new
    each day in his bathtub
The Founding Fathers   Major Douglas   Gesell   Frobenius and Del Mar
    Gaudier and Wyndham
Homer and Divus   Ovid, the magician   Propertius, "with a crowd of
    young women doing homage to his palaver"
An odd fellow named Mauberley, who didn't quite know who he was

Who is the speaker?
Who is it that is telling us everything that ever happened?
The speaker is "No Man"—and Jedermann.
Ego scriptor   sic locutus est
Has he entered the great acorn of light?

*   *   *

Let me try to recall for you some of the writers who were in Pound's head when, without any books to consult, he wrote Canto 74, the first of *The Pisan Cantos*. Where possible, I'll quote a few lines in the original language because that was what Pound was hearing. Call this exercise what you will—it should fix his canon for us, his tradition.

Eliot

The reference to Eliot and his poem *The Hollow Men*, which was published in 1925, is on *page 425, line 9*:

> yet say this to the Possum: a bang, not a whimper

In their correspondence, Eliot is "Old Possum" and Pound is "Br'er Rabbit," these from the Uncle Remus stories of Joel Chandler Harris. Pound was often a trial, but Eliot stuck by him to the end. He lobbied the other judges to help Pound win the Bollingen Prize for *The Pisan Cantos* in 1949 and often visited him at St. Elizabeths.

Eliot's poem begins: "We are the hollow men / We are the stuffed men / Leaning together / Headpiece filled with straw . . ." and it ends: *"This is the way the world ends / Not with a bang but a whimper." The Hollow Men* is, of course, a religious poem. Pound liked to call Eliot an "Anglo-Cat" and sometimes addressed him as the Reverend Eliot.

Dioce and Herodotus

Pound drew on Herodotus's account of the city that was built by Deioces, a king of the Medes when he wrote on *page* 425, *line* 11:

To build the city of Dioce whose terraces are the colour of stars.

Dioce had great significance for Pound; it stood for the *paradiso terrestre,* the earthly paradise, to which he hoped his theories of economic and social reform would lead.

Pound read Herodotus in English—his copy is at his daughter Mary's castle in the Italian Tyrol, so we can dispense with the Greek.

Once firmly on the throne, Deioces put pressure on the Medes to build a single great city to which, as the capital of the country, all other towns were to be held of secondary importance. Again they complied, and the city now known as Ecbatana was built, a place of great size and strength fortified by concentric walls, these so planned that each successive circle was higher than the one below it by the height of the battlements. The fact that it was built on a hill helped to bring about this effect, but still more was done by deliberate contrivance. The circles are seven in number, and the innermost contains the royal palace and treasury. The circuit of the outer wall is much the same in extent as at Athens. The battlements of the five outer rings are painted in different colours, the first white, the second black, the third crimson, the fourth blue, the fifth orange; the battlements of the two inner rings are plated with silver and gold respectively.

Notice how Pound's line improves on Herodotus to get a sound effect. Pound had a great ear for putting words together. Herodotus's "rings plated with silver and gold" is not very lovely as sound. Pound's "colour of stars" is. See how he has used the *rs*. As you go through the *Cantos* you will find many instances where an adjective seems illogical. But if you study it, you'll see the word is there for the sound. Take the "gonads" in a line from Canto 21:

> Floating flame in the air, gonads in organdy

A flame seldom floats, but the two "fl" sounds are fine together. "Gonads in organdy" is rather absurd, but Pound has put "gon" and "gan" together to good effect.

Wagadu and Frobenius

The reference to Frobenius and his myth of Wagadu is found on *page 430, lines 27–32*:

> 4 times was the city rebuilded, Hooo Fasa
> Gassir, Hooo Fasa dell' Italia tradita
> now in the mind indestructible, Gassir, Hoooo Fasa,
> With the four giants at the four corners
> and four gates mid-wall Hooo Fasa
> and a terrace the colour of stars.

The German anthropologist Leo Frobenius (1873–1938) found the myth of Wagadu in an oral Sudanese Soninke legend called "Gassire's Lute." It is translated by Douglas Fox in his collection *African Genesis*. Fox was on the staff of Frobenius's Forschungs-Institut in Frankfurt and became Pound's friend and mine.

> Four times Wagadu stood there in all her splendor. Four times
> Wagadu disappeared and was lost to human sight: once through

vanity, once through falsehood, once through greed and once through dissension. Four times Wagadu changed her name. First she was called Dierra, then Agada, then Ganna, then Silla. Four times she turned her face. Once to the north, once to the west, once to the east and once to the south. For Wagadu, whenever men have seen her, has always had four gates: one to the north, one to the west, one to the east and one to the south. Those are the directions whence the strength of Wagadu comes, the strength in which she endures no matter whether she be built of stone, wood and earth or lives but as a shadow in the mind and longing of her children. For really, Wagadu is not of stone, not of wood, not of earth. Wagadu is the strength which lives in the hearts of men and is sometimes visible because eyes see her and ears hear the clash of swords and ring of shields, and is sometimes invisible because the indomitability of men has overtired her, so that she sleeps. Sleep came to Wagadu for the first time through vanity, for the second time through falsehood, for the third time through greed and for the fourth time through dissension. Should Wagadu ever be found for the fourth time, then she will live so forcefully in the minds of men that she will never be lost again, so forcefully that vanity, falsehood, greed and dissension will never be able to harm her.

Hoooh! Dierra, Agada, Ganna, Silla! Hoooh! Fasa!

A great teacher draws us to writers off the beaten track whom he has discovered, revealing qualities of thought and style that we would not otherwise have found. In the *ABC of Reading* Pound posits that the best literature has been done, in this sequence, by the inventors (men who found a new process), the masters (men who combined a number of such processes), and the diluters (men who came after the first two kinds). As his critical books show, Pound searched constantly for the inventors of his canon.

Pound believed that Frobenius was an inventor in his field. He magnified Frobenius into a kind of personal myth, an ikon of how the scientific mind should function. Frobenius became as important for Pound as Louis Agassiz the naturalist.[2] Pound worked some of Frobenius's theories of *Paideuma*, which he defined as the "tangle of or complex of inrooted ideas of any period," into his own thinking on the "traditional culture of a people" in *Guide to Kulchur*. While Pound read some German, he did not follow anthropology. I think he must have heard about Frobenius in the late 1920s from Douglas Fox.

Frobenius's special subjects were primitive African art—on his expeditions he discovered important cave pictographs in different parts of Africa—and tribal legends surviving from primitive times. Pound was intrigued with the way Frobenius did not relegate his findings to history but related them to living traditions of folklore and native religions.

Frobenius's masterwork (in seven volumes) is the *Erlebte Erdteile* (Parts of the World Experienced). It has never been translated into English, nor has the shorter *Kulturgeschichte Afrikas* (Cultural History of Africa). American anthropologists such as Margaret Mead and Ruth Benedict did not take Frobenius seriously—a fact that enraged Pound. But he was taken seriously by Jung in *The Psychology of the Unconscious* and by Oswald Spengler in *The Decline of the West*—perhaps a dubious distinction? The poet Apollinaire knew Frobenius's reproductions of primitive African art.

Frobenius's science was *Kulturmorphologie*, which Pound translated as "the transformation of cultures." Here are some quotations from Pound's *Guide to Kulchur*:

> The value of Leo Frobenius to civilization is not for the rightness or wrongness of this opinion or that opinion but for the kind of thinking he does.
>
> He has in especial seen and marked out a kind of knowing, the difference between knowledge that has to be acquired by particular effort and knowing that is in people "in the air." He has accented the value of such record. His archaeology is not retrospective, it is immediate.
>
> Paideuma is the grisly roots of ideas that are in action.

Pound's favorite Frobenius stories are the ones that show how his mind worked: Some African villagers needed a new well. Where to dig? Frobenius located the right spot near a cave with pictographs. There had to have been underground water there in prehistoric times. Another story from *Guide to Kulchur*:

> Frobenius forgets his notebook, ten miles from camp he remembers it. Special African feast on, and no means of sketching it for the records. No time to return to camp. No matter. Black starts drumming. Drum telegraph works and sketching materials arrive in time for the beano.

Should we not compare this kind of mental process with the famous story about Agassiz, another one of Pound's intellectual heroes, who appears in the *Cantos* on pages 598, 625, 635, 716, 732, 762, and 786. The story is on page 17 of the *ABC of Reading*, where Pound writes:

> The proper METHOD for studying poetry and good letters is the method of contemporary biologists, that is careful first-hand examination of the matter, and continual COMPARISON of one 'slide' or specimen with another.
>
> No man is equipped for modern thinking until he has understood the anecdote of Agassiz and the fish:
>
> A post-graduate student equipped with honours and diplomas went to Agassiz to receive the final and finishing touches. The great man offered him a small fish and told him to describe it.
>
> Post-graduate student: 'That's only a sunfish.'
>
> Agassiz: 'I know that. Write a description of it.'
>
> After a few minutes the student returned with a description of the Ichthus Heliodiplodokus, or whatever term is used to conceal the common sunfish from vulgar knowledge, family of Heliichtherinkus, etc., as found in textbooks of the subject.
>
> Agassiz again told the student to describe the fish.
>
> The student produced a four-page essay. Agassiz then told him to look at the fish. At the end of three weeks the fish was in an

advanced state of decomposition, but the student knew something about it.

The best commentary I know on Pound's link with Frobenius is
that by Guy Davenport in the symposium *Motives & Method in
the Cantos of Ezra Pound*, edited by Lewis Leary (Columbia, 1954).
Frobenius appears on pages 189, 427, 442, 574, 598, and 729 of
the *Cantos*.

The Odyssey

Starting with a quote in the original Greek, the reference to the
Odyssey is on *page 425, lines 22–23*:

> ΟΎ ΤΙΣ, ΟΎ ΤΙΣ? Odysseus
> the name of my family.

ΟΎ ΤΙΣ or Ou tis (I am no one)—or as Robert Fitzgerald translates it to get the Greek pun, "I am Nohbdy"—is what Odysseus
answers when the Cyclops Polyphemus asks him his name. The
myth is in Book IX of the *Odyssey*. Odysseus and a dozen of his
crew are trapped in the cave of the one-eyed giant, who begins
to make a meal of them. But Odysseus outwits him. He tells him
that his name is "No Man," then gets him drunk and puts out
the single eye with a spike heated in the fire. Polyphemus cries
for help but tells his comrade giants that "No man is killing me,"
so they go away. Odysseus and his men escape from the cave by
clinging to the bellies of the blinded giant's rams.

Pound always read the *Odyssey* in Greek so I'll give you a few
lines for the flavor of the words. Odysseus is telling Polyphemus that his name is "No Man," that all his friends and family
call him that. He asks for a gift the giant has promised.

> Κύκλωψ, εἰρωτάϊς μ'ὄνομα κλυτόν, αὐτὰρ ἐγώ τοι
> ἐξερέω, σὺ ὑέ μοι δὸς ξείνιον, ὥς περ ὑπέςτης
> Οὖτις ἐμοί γ'ὄνομα, Οὖτιν δέ με κικλήςκονςι
> μήτηρ ἠδὲ πατὴρ ἠδ' ἄλλοι πάντες ἑταῖροι.

Kyklops eirontais m'onoma kluton autar ego toi
Exereo su de moi dos xeinion os per upestes
Outis emoi g'onoma outin de me kikleskousi
Meter ede pater ed'alloi pantes etairoi.

You will have noticed that on page 430, where there is a re-
peat of "Ou tis," Pound has placed a Chinese character beside
it. He often did this when he wished to compare or ratify a concept in Western culture with something from the East. This is a
function of the ideogrammatic method. The character
here is *Mo* (character #4557 in Matthews' Chinese dictionary[3])—"a negative; not; no"—which corresponds
to the negative of "Ou tis." David Gordon explains that this
character originally represented vegetation covering the sun, to
give the idea of "nightfall" or "sundown," as we see it in a Yin
dynasty sacrificial bone drawing. But the grass beneath the sun
later came to be mistaken for the drawing of a human figure, so
that Pound saw the human shape beneath a grass covered sun
and read: "a man on whom the sun has gone down," which for
him corresponded to "no man" or "Ou tis."

The "Aged Snow"; Sappho and Catullus

The "aged Snow" was an Oxford don with whom Pound argued
in 1913 about the relative merits of Sappho and Catullus. The
reference to Snow and the poets is found on *page 444, lines*
31–35:

> He said I protested too much   he wanted to start a press
> and print the greek classics . . . periplum
>   and the very *very* aged Snow created considerable
> hilarity quoting the φαίνε-τ-τ-τ-τττ-αί μοι
> in reply to *l'aer tremare*

The tag in Greek is from Sappho's most famous poem, the
"phainetai moi kenos isos theoisin," and the one in Italian is
from Cavalcanti's Sonnet 7, which Pound translated.

For the sound of it, here is the first stanza of the Sappho. This has come down to us whole because the rhetorician Longinus admired it so much that he quoted it entire in his treatise *On the Sublime*.

> φαίνεταί μοι κῆνος ἴσος θέοῖσιν
> ἔμμεν' ὠνήρ, ὄστις εναντίος τοι
> ἰζάνει καὶ πλησίον ἁδὺ φωνεύσας ὑπακούει

> phainetai moi kenos isos theoisin
> 'emmen oner, 'ottis enantios toi
> isdanei kai plasion adu phoncisas upakouei

Pound did not publish any translations of Sappho, but his friend William Carlos Williams did a beautiful version which he incorporated in *Paterson* at the beginning of Book V, Part II. Williams didn't know much Greek but got help on his translation from a professor friend. Here is the Williams Sappho:

> Peer of the gods is that man, who
> face to face, sits listening
> to your sweet speech and lovely
>   laughter.

> It is this that rouses a tumult
> in my breast. At mere sight of you
> my voice falters, my tongue
>   is broken.

> Straightway, a delicate fire runs in
> my limbs; my eyes
> are blinded and my ears
>   thunder.

> Sweat pours out; a trembling hunts
> me down. I grow paler

than dry grass and lack little
of dying.

A great poem, as the "phanetai moi" is, can enter the stream of tradition. Catullus knew it and rewrote it closely in Latin, reproducing Sappho's meters. This is how Catullus's first stanza sounds in Latin:

Ille mi par esse deo videtur,
Ille, si fas est, superare divos,
qui sedens adversus identidem te
        spectat et audit
dulce ridentem.[4]

In the course of tradition some odd things can happen. One of the curiosities of the modernist movement is Louis Zukofsky's "phonetic" version of Catullus 51. He set out to reproduce in English the actual sounds of the Latin words—without too much concern for syntax or simple English meaning. The effect is somewhat monstrous, certainly not Catullus and not typical Zukofsky.

He'll hie me, par is he? the God divide her,
he'll hie, see fastest, superior deity,
quiz—sitting adverse identity—mate, in-
        spect it and audit—
you'll care ridden then....

There are two references to Catullus in Canto 74. On *page 427, lines* 16–19 Pound writes:

and the water was still on the West side
flowing toward the Villa Catullo
where with sound ever moving
        in diminutive poluphloisboios

Pound is talking about Sirmione, the romantic little peninsula that juts out into Lake Garda. Sirmione was his favorite vacation spot in Italy. Before they were married, he went there with Dorothy, chaperoned, of course, by her mother, the novelist Olivia Shakespear, who was one of the mistesses of Yeats. It was there that he first met Joyce. Some Roman ruins out at the end of the point are thought to be "Catullus's Villa," because of Catullus's poem (Number 31) which begins:

> Paene insularum, Sirmio, insularumque
> ocelle . . .

> Sirmio, dearest gem of islands and of almost islands . . .

The other reference is on *page 428, line 5*:

> Butterflies, mint and Lesbia's sparrows . . .

This refers to Catullus's famous poem about his girlfriend's pet sparrow:

> Passer, deliciae meae puellae,
> quicum ludere, quem in sinu tenere,
> cui primum digitum dare appetenti
> et acris solet incitare morsus . . .

which Horace Gregory renders somewhat freely:

> Sparrow, O sweet sparrow,
> love of my lady love,
> she who's always nursing
> you between her breasts and
> feeding you her fingertips . . .

Pound himself translated only three short poems of Catullus, of which Number 43, "To Formianus' Young Lady Friend," is an adaptation in the bantering tone of parts of the *Propertius*.

> All Hail; young lady with a nose—
>   by no means too small,
> With a foot unbeautiful,
>   and with eyes that are not black,
> With fingers that are not long, and with a mouth undry,
> And with a tongue by no means too elegant,
> You are the friend of Formianus, the vendor of cosmetics,
> And they call you beautiful in the province,
> And you are even compared to Lesbia.
>
> O most unfortunate age!

Number 85, the famous "Odi et Amo," the love-hate epigram, may have appealed to Pound by its brevity, reminding him of the short poems of some of his Imagist friends. But Catullus was not writing an Imagist (or haiku) poem. "In a Station of the Metro" has fourteen words. Pound's "Odi et Amo" has twenty.

> Odi et amo, quare id faciam, fortasse requiris.
>   nescio, sed fieri sentio et excrucior.
>
> I hate and love. Why? You may ask but
> It beats me. I feel it done to me, and ache.

Cavalcanti

At Oxford, Pound had tried to convince "the aged Snow" that Cavalcanti was as good as Sappho. "L'aer tremare" (making the air to tremble [when she comes]) is the second line of Cavalcanti's Sonnet VII, which you will find in Pound's *Translations* volume. Here is the Italian of the first two stanzas:

Chi è questa che vien, ch' ogni uom la mira,
Che fa di clarità l' aer tremare,
E mena seco Amor, sí che parlare
Null' uom ne puote, ma ciascun sospira?

Ahi, Dio, che sembra quando gli occhi gira?
Dicalo Amor, ch' io nol saprei contare:
Cotanto d'umiltà donna mi pare,
Che ciascun' altra in vêr di lei chiam' ira.

And here is Pound:

Who is she that comes, makyng turn every man's eye
And makyng the air to tremble with a bright clearenesse
That leadeth with her Love, in such nearness
No man may proffer of speech more than a sigh?

Ah God, what she is like when her owne eye turneth, is
Fit for Amor to speake, for I can not at all;
Such is her modesty, I would call
Every woman else but an useless uneasiness.

Pound had an almost inordinate admiration for Guido Cavalcanti. Cavalcanti was always in Pound's mind, not only for the
beauty of his verse, but also for the clarity of his thought. About
1941, during the war and before his incarceration at Pisa, Pound
wrote two cantos in Italian, the so-called "missing cantos," 72
and 73. These have only recently been published in a new printing of the New Directions collection. Canto 73 has the form of a
dream in which Pound meets the shade of Cavalcanti riding on
horseback. In the translation by his daughter Mary de Rachewiltz it begins:

And then I slept, and upon awakening in the dark I saw and
heard, and him I saw seemed to be on horseback, and I heard:
    It gives me no pleasure to see my people dying steeped in mud
and shame, governed by carrion and foresworne. Roosevelt,

Churchill and Eden, bastards and yidds, rogues and liars all of them, and the people squeezed and foolish.

Dead as I was in Sarzaba, now I wait for the call of the rising. I am that Guido you loved for his proud spirit and clarity. Of the third heaven I know the radiance, on horseback (never postillion) I went through the streets of the town, otherwise called the doleful city [Florence], always torn, her people mean and fickle, a bunch of slaves.

I'll spare you most of the rest of Canto 73. It is, to say the least, unappetizing. It tells the story, which Pound must have gotten from a newspaper clipping, of a "heroic" young Fascist girl scout, "una contadinella, un po' tozza ma bella" ("a little peasant, a bit chunky but beautiful") who leads a company of Canadian soldiers onto a minefield and they are all blown up.

> Out of sheer love, a heroine. Defying death, she conquered her strange fate.

And Cavalcanti/Pound ends the canto:

> Glory of our country!... I have come back from the third heaven to see Romagna, to see the mountains during the rising.... In the North our country is reborn. What a girl! Those girls, those boys, they wear black!

What a sad and tragic poem, considering what Pound once had been. I see it as a sign of incipient dementia.

The Troubadours

There is only one reference to the troubadours in Canto 74, on *page* 428, *lines* 8–10, which Pound has composed in Provençal:

> el triste pensier si volge
> ad Ussel. A Ventadour
> va il consire, el tempo rivolge

        (the sad thought turns
            toward Ussel. To Ventadour
                goes the thought, the time turns back.)

This refers to the troubadour Bernart de Ventadorn, whose "The Lark" and "Quant l'herbe fresq el fuell apar" Pound translated. In *The Spirit of Romance* Pound gives us part of the *vida* of Bernart, that he "was of Limousin, of the castle of Ventadorn, and was one of low degree, son, to wit, of a serving-man who gathered brushwood for the heating of the oven wherein was baked the castle bread." Not all of the troubadours were born noble; with enough talent they could make it—and with the noble ladies.

We do not know how either *langue d'oc*, the poetic language of the south of France, or *langue d'oil*, that of the north in which the *chansons de geste* were written, were pronounced. The best one can do is to listen to the speech of the troubadours' descendants, now called Occitan. *Langue d'oc* is a curious tongue. Basically it is a romance language, kin to French, Italian, Spanish, and Catalan, but most of the words sound quite different. They tend to be short with many jagged *s*, *z*, and *tz* endings. It sounds a bit like the Romansch dialect of the Grisons in Switzerland. Here are the opening lines of "The Lark":

        Can vei la lauzeta mover
        de joi sas alas contral rai,
        que s'oblid' es laissa chazer
        per la doussor c'al cor li vai,
        ai! tan grans enveya m'en ve
        de cui qu'eu veya jauzion.

And here is Pound's version of them:

        When I see the lark a-moving
        For joy his wings against the sunlight,
        Who forgets himself and lets himself fall
        For the sweetness which goes into his heart;

> Ai! what great envy comes unto me for him whom
>> I see so rejoicing!

Dante

There are two tags from Dante, the most colorful one, *page 436, lines 5–7*, referring to the cruel story of Ugolino della Gherardesca, whom we meet in Canto 33 of the *Inferno*.

> To the left of la bella Torre the tower of Ugolino
>> in the tower to the left of the tower
>>> chewed his son's head

Dante and Virgil find Ugolino in the circle of ice, among the traitors. He had lost out in the factional struggle between the Guelfs and the Ghibellines when he tried to take over the city of Pisa and, with two sons and two grandsons, was imprisoned in what came to be known as the Tower of Famine. After some months the door of their cell was nailed shut and they were left to starve to death. In "chewed his son's head," Pound seems to be accepting the legend of cannibalism, though Dante says only "ripreso 'l teschio misero co' denti" (he seized on the unfortunate skull with his teeth), that is he says "skull" not "head." Dante's Italian sounds very different from that of Cavalcanti. Dante eschews the internal rhymes of some of the other poets of the *dolce stil nuovo*, giving us his resounding *terza rima*, tercets in which line 2 of each triad rhymes with 1 and 3 of the next— *aba / bcb / cdc*. Dante gets great power from condensation; there is much elision and truncation of words. Cavalcanti is rhetorical and abstract; Dante is concrete with a great deal of specificity in his descriptions. The piteous tale of Ugolino and his children is one of the great set pieces of the *Commedia*; we can see in some of the "horror stories" of the *Cantos* how much Pound had it in mind.

> Quivi morì; e come tu mi vedi,
>> vid' io cascar li tre ad uno ad uno

tra 'l quinto dì e 'l sesto; ond' io mi diedi,
Già cieco, a brancolar sovra ciascuno,
   e due dì li chiamai, poi che fur morti:
   poscia, più che 'l dolor, potè 'l digiuno.
Quand' ebbe detto ciò, con li occhi torti
   riprese 'l teschio misero co' denti,
   che furo all' osso, come d' un can, forti.

I'll give the high point of the story in Laurence Binyon's translation because Pound collaborated on it. In the *Letters* volume you will find a number of letters to Binyon in which Pound advises him on how to handle Dante's prosody and tone, with detailed comments on many lines.

A cranny of light crept in upon the stone
   Of that dungeon of woe; and I saw there
   On those four faces the aspect of my own.
I bit upon both hands in my despair.
   And they supposing it was in the access
   Of hunger, rose up with a sudden prayer,
And said, 'O Father, it will hurt much less
   If you of us eat: take what once you gave
   To clothe us, this flesh of our wretchedness.'
Thereon I calmed myself, their grief to save.
   That day and the one after we were dumb.
   Hard earth, couldst thou not open for our grave?
But when to the fourth morning we were come,
   Gaddo at my feet stretched himself with a cry:
   'Father, why won't you help me?' and lay numb
And there died. Ev'n as thou seest me, saw I,
   One after the other, the three fall. They drew,
   Between the fifth and sixth day, their last sigh.
I, blind now, groping arms about them threw,
   And still called on them that were two days dead.
   Then fasting did what anguish could not do."
He ceased, and with eyes twisted in his head

His teeth seized on the lamentable skull
Strong as a dog's upon a bony shred.

Villon

We have two fragmentary quotations from Villon: *page 427, lines 31–32:*

under *les six potences*
Absouldre, que tous nous vueil absoudre

(under the six gallows trees,
[pray god] that he will absolve us all)

[The refrain from Villon's "Epitaphe"]

The other is from *page 436, line 12:*

pouvrette et ancienne oncques lettres ne lus

(poor and old and never learned to read)

Villon was one of Pound's heroes. When he decided to compose an opera he took lines from Villon for his libretto, which was in French, and called it *Le Testament.* (His second opera is based on the poems of Cavalcanti.) In a chapter devoted to Villon in *The Spirit of Romance,* he says of him that he had "no care whatever for the flowery traditions of medieval art" and "preferred unvarnished intimate speech, that what he saw he wrote, never forgetting his fascinating, revolting self, and that he was a voice of suffering, of mockery, of irrevocable fact." His work, Pound concluded, "is a lurid canto of the *Inferno,* written too late to be included in the original text."

Except for some fragments in *The Spirit of Romance,* Pound did not translate Villon. So for the passage I'd like to show, I'll use the translation by Rossetti, which Pound uses in *The Spirit of Romance.* This is from the ballade "Dame du ciel" (Lady of

Heaven), which is interesting for us because it includes not only the "pouvrette et ancienne oncques lettre ne lus" of Canto 74 but also the "paradis paint ou sont harpes et luz" of Canto 45:

> with usura
> hath no man a painted paradise on his church wall
> *harpes et luz*

Here is the French of the third stanza of "Dame du ciel":

> Femme je suis pouvrette et ancienne
> Qui riens ne sçay, oncques lettre ne lus,
> Au moustier voy dont suis paroissienne
> Paradis paint ou sont harpes et lus
> Et ung enfer ou dampnez sont boullus:
> L'ung me fait paour, l'autre joye et liesse,
> La joye avoir me fay, haulte Deesse,
> A qui pecheurs doivent tous recourir
> Comblez de foy, sans fainte ne paresse,
> En ceste foy je vueil vivre et mourir.

And here is Rossetti's English version:

> A pitiful poor woman, shrunk and old,
> I am, and nothing learned in letter-lore,
> Within my parish-cloister I behold
> A painted Heaven where harps and lutes adore,
> And eke an Hell whose damned folk seethe full sore:
> One bringeth fear, the other joy to me.
> That joy, great goddess, make thou mine to be, —
> Thou of whom all must ask it even as I;
> And that which faith desires, that let it see,
> For in this faith I choose to live and die.

Heine

Except for the Minnesingers, the German troubadours, Pound was not too much interested in German poetry. (His two translations of Walther von der Vogelweide are in *Forked Branches*.) He never read Rilke, so far as I know, and, early on, he dismissed Goethe with this: that "when the joys of taxidermy sufficed not to maintain his self-respect, he was wont to rejoice that there was something noble and divine in being *Kuenstler*." Later, however, he admitted that "his lyrics are so fine, so unapproachable... but outside his lyrics he never comes off his perch." But Pound did like Heine, for whom our tag in Canto 74 is somewhat tangential, *page* 441, *line* 9, where he speaks of seeing the *Gedichte* of Heine on the parlor shelf of Frau Unterguggenberger, the wife of the Burgomeister in Wörgl, the Austrian town where Gesell's stampscrip was tried out. Pound said of Heine that he had a "clear palette" and that he knew how to put in the "bitters." Since some of them are more adaptations than translations, Pound did not put his Heine versions in the *Translations* volume; they are in *Personae*. And here he has a charming little salutation, "Translator to Translated":

> O Harry Heine, curses be,
> I live too late to sup with thee!
> Who can demolish at such polished ease
> Philistia's pomp and Art's pomposities!

The jocularity of that greeting carries into "This delightful young man," a close translation of Heine's *Heimkehr* 65:

> Diesen liebenswürdigen Jüngling
> Kann man nicht genug verehren;
> Oft traktiert er mich mit Austern,
> Und mit Rheinwein und Likören.
>
> Zierlich sitzt ihm Rock und Höschen,
> Doch noch zierlicher die Binde,

Und so kommt er jeden Morgen,
Fragt, ob ich mich wohlbefinde;

Spricht von meinem weiten Ruhme,
Meiner Anmut, meinen Witzen;
Eifrig und geschäftig ist er
Mir zu dienen, mir zu nützen.

Und des Abends, in Gesellschaft,
Mit begeistertem Gesichte,
Deklamiert er vor den Damen
Meine göttlichen Gedichte.

O wie ist es hoch erfreulich,
Solchen Jüngling noch zu finden,
Jetzt in unsrer Zeit, wo täglich
Mehr und mehr die Bessern schwinden.

Pound lets out all the stops of his comicality and has fun with
the rhymes, reproducing Heine's scheme exactly, down to the
humorously impure triple rhyme in the first stanza.

This delightful young man
Should not lack for honourers,
He propitiates me with oysters,
With Rhine wine and liqueurs.

How his coat and pants adorn him!
Yet his ties are more adorning,
In these he daily comes to ask me:
"Are you feeling well this morning?"

He speaks of my extended fame,
My wit, charm, definitions,
And is diligent to serve me,
Is detailed in his provisions.

In evening company he sets his face
In most spiritu*el* positions,
And declaims before the ladies
My *god-like* compositions.

O what comfort is it for me
To find him such, when the days bring
No comfort, at my time of life when
All good things go vanishing.

(In hunting up Heine's text I ran into something I had forgotten, if I ever knew it: Heine wrote a little poem in praise of Bertran de Born, but it is so stiff it wouldn't have appealed to Pound.)

Verlaine

Pound translated four poems by Rimbaud but he does not recall him in Canto 74. However there is a reference to Verlaine on *page* 449, *lines* 1–3:

Serenely in the crystal jet
     as the bright ball that the fountain tosses
(Verlaine) as diamond clearness

Kenner explains that "the one word 'Verlaine' assembles 'crystal' and 'jet' and sculptor [he means the sculptor seeing form in the air in Canto 2] under the sign of his 'Clair de Lune' which closes with great ecstatic fountains among statues..." Here is Verlaine's "Clair de Lune":

CLAIR DE LUNE

Votre âme est un paysage choisi
Que vont charmant masques et bergamasques,
Jouant du luth et dansant et quasi
Tristes sous leurs déguisements fantasques.

Tout en chantant sur le mode mineur
L'amour vainqueur et la vie opportune,
Ils n'ont pas l'air de croire à leur bonheur,
Et leur chanson se mêle au clair de lune,

Au calme clair de lune triste et beau,
Qui fait rêver les oiseaux dans les arbres
Et sangloter d'extase les jets d'eau,
Les grands jets d'eau sveltes parmi les marbres.

Here is the period translation of Arthur Symons, who was contemporary with Verlaine. With all that has happened since in poetry, Verlaine sounds rather corny now, but we should remember that when he wrote he was breaking new ground, and the mellifluousness of his language is miraculous in the French.

CLAIR DE LUNE

(Fêtes Galantes.)

Your soul is a sealed garden, and there go
With masque and bergamasque fair companies
Playing on lutes and dancing as though
Sad under their fantastic fripperies.

Though they in minor keys go carolling
Of love the conqueror and of live boon
They seem to doubt the happiness they sing
And the song melts into the light of the moon,

The sad light of the moon, so lovely fair
That all the birds dream in the leafy shade
And the slim fountains sob into the air
Among the marble statues in the glade.

Ben Jonson

There were, of course, ever so many English poems in Pound's head when he was writing *The Pisan Cantos*. Some of these were recalled to him by the paperback anthology of poetry, Morris Speare's *Pocket Book of Verse,* which he found in the camp privy.

> That from the gates of death,
>> that from the gates of death: Whitman or Lovelace
>> found on the jo-house seat at that
> in a cheap edition! [and thanks to Professor Speare]

> (CANTO 80, page 513)

One of the most beautiful poems in Speare is Ben Jonson's "Her Triumph," and our reference is on *page* 449, *lines* 14–15:

> Hast 'ou seen the rose in the steel dust
>> (or swansdown ever?)

The "rose in the steel dust" is not in the poem—Pound seems to have gotten that from Allen Upward's *The New Word,* but he echoes Jonson's "Hast 'ou" for "Hast thou" as early as Canto 47—showing that it was in his head long before he read Speare —and in three other cantos.

HER TRIUMPH

> See the chariot at hand here of Love
>> Wherein my lady rideth!
> Each that draws is a swan or a dove,
>> And well the car Love guideth;
> As she goes all hearts do duty
>> Unto her beauty;
> And enamoured do wish, so they might
>> But enjoy such a sight,

That they still were to run by her side
Through swords, through seas, whither she would ride.

Do but look on her eyes, they do light
   All that Love's world compriseth!
Do but look on her hair, it is bright
   As Love's star when it riseth!
Do but mark, her forehead's smoother
      Than words that soothe her!
And from her arched brows such a grace
      Sheds itself through her face,
As alone there triumphs to the life
All the gain, all the good, of the elements' strife.

Have you seen but a bright lily grow
   Before rude hands have touched it?
Ha' you marked but the fall o' the snow
   Before the soil has smutched it?
Ha' you felt the wool of beaver
   Or swan's down ever?
Or have smelt o' the bud o' the briar?
   Or the nard in the fire?
Or have tasted the bag of the bee?
O so white! O so soft! O so sweet is she!

Confucius

The only books that Pound brought to the Disciplinary Training
Center were Legge's text of Confucius and a Chinese dictionary.
He was allowed to keep them because he told the guards they
had to do with his religoin. On *page 426, lines 24–27* we find:

not words whereto to be faithful
   nor deeds that they be resolute
      only that bird-hearted equity make timber
      and lay hold of the earth

These lines, David Gordon tells me, "refer to one of Pound's favorite chapters from Mencius: 'The great man does not think before-hand of his words that they may be sincere, nor of his actions that they may be resolute; he simply *speaks and does* what is right' (Mencius IV, 2, xi; the Legge translation).

Then on *page 437, lines 26–34* we have:

> To study with the white wings of time passing
>> is not that our delight
> to have friends come from far countries
>> is not that pleasure
> nor to care that we are untrumpeted?
>>> filial, fraternal affection is the root of humaneness
>> the root of the process
> nor are elaborate speeches and slick alacrity.

This passage is from the opening of Book I of the *Analects*. The first four lines are fairly close to Pound's translation in *Confucius* but then imagination and wit take off to make the lines more poetic. "Unruffled by men's ignoring him" in the prose becomes "nor to care that we are untrumpeted." "Elaborate phrasing" in the prose becomes "elaborate speeches and slick alacrity." Do you hear in these alterations, as I do, an echo of the witty tone of the *Homage to Sextus Propertius*?

Once when I was visiting him at St. Elizabeths, Pound "sang" me some Chinese. He had, in his way, mastered the tones — Chinese is spoken with four different voice tones — and he gave a good performance, an up-and-down singsong. He took the language so seriously as to mark up a transliteration of the three hundred pages of *Confucian Odes*, showing in which tone each character should be sung to produce a melodic line. He called this his "singing text"; it has never been published. The tone helps to identify the meaning of a character. Thus there are, in the characters used in the *Cantos*, three different "ho"s, four "pi"s, two "yueh"s, and five "li"s. Occasionally Pound will set the tone numbers beside the characters, as on page 595. Gordon points out "how Pound's etymologies are aptly reconciled to the last four climactic ideograms of Mencius: ('what is right')

惟 ("heart," "bird") "only"

義 "equity"

所 ("door," "axe") "make timber"

在 ("hand holding earth") "lay hold of earth"

Noh Plays

There are two references to the Japanese Noh plays that Pound adapted from the notebooks of Ernest Fenollosa; one to the *Hagoromo* on *page 430, lines 10–11*:

> and the nymph of the Hagoromo came to me,
> as a corona of angels

and one to the *Kagekiyo* and *Kumasaka* on *page 442, lines 15–17*:

> remembering Kagekiyo: "how stiff the shaft of your neck is."
> and they went off each his own way
> "a better fencer than I was," said Kumasaka, a shade

Kagekiyo's words are almost literal from the text in Pound's *Classic Noh Theatre of Japan*, page 111. The chorus is recounting a hand-to-hand fight between Kagekiyo and his rival Miyonoya. Kumasaka's "a better fencer than I was" is Pound's recollection of his line in the play (page 42) "they had no rivals in fencing," where Kumasaka is praising the fighting skill of his comrades in arms.

I have heard it said, though Pound did not say it to me, that when he was planning his operas, *Le Testament* and *Cavalcanti*, Pound had the Noh plays in mind. I can't see much connection. The operas are not ritualistic. If you look at the cast of characters in many Noh plays you will find a personage called Kyogen,

who is described as "of the place" or "a local person." The inter-
ludes of the Kyogen are not in the exalted poetic style of the
main characters. The Kyogen talks colloquially and is often a
clown. Some authorities call him comic relief, like the clowns in
Shakespeare or the knocking at the gate in *Macbeth*, used to
break the tension and the slow pace of the serious drama. Others say that the Kyogen was intended to amuse the groundlings
while the ceremonial characters changed their elaborate cos-
tumes between scenes. Pound, following Fenollosa, did not
designate Kyogens, but he knew about them. Once when I asked
him if he had ever written stories, he told me that he had done a
"Kyogen" about two policemen—but he hoped it was lost.

Well, it isn't lost. Donald Gallup has recently turned up *The
Protagonist* along with four other playlets, in the Pound Archive
at Yale. I'm sorry to report that, to me, it is boring. Apparently it
was written when Pound was living with Yeats in the Stone Cottage in Sussex in 1913. The coppers speak Irish brogue. The
Noh plays made a profound impression on Yeats, who was already obsessed with spirits. They reshaped his dramaturgy. He
conceived of an aristocratic form—a bare stage, as in the Noh,
masks, ritual dance to the sound of rhythmic instruments, and a
chorus extraneous from the action. *At the Hawk's Well* and *The
Dreaming of the Bones* are examples of these Yeats "plays for
dancers."

Other playwrights have been influenced by the Noh—Claudel
for his marionette plays, Brecht in *Der Jasager und der Neinsager*,
and even Tennessee Williams, coached by his friend Yukio Mi-
shima, thought of his *Clothes for a Summer Hotel*, a play about the
Fitzgeralds where Hemingway appears from the dead, as a
"ghost play."

Earl Miner tells us that the Noh showed Pound "how to write
a long Vorticist, (that is, imagist) poem since he saw in it a technique by which critical images unified whole plays or passages.
He utilized . . . this technique of 'Unity of Image' in the *Cantos* by
employing certain recurring archetypal images . . . to unify the
poem." This is a simplification of the structure of the *Cantos*, but
the link with the Noh is interesting.

And so it goes. There are many other literary echoes in Canto
74 on which I have not touched: The Taoists, Plotinus, St. Francis, Scotus Erigena, the Bible, Lenin, his friend the poet Basil
Bunting, Ford, Yeats, Joyce, Virgil, Pythagoras, Allen Upward,
St. John of the Cross, Baudelaire, Sophocles, John Adams, Aristotle, Lady Murasaki, Francis Thompson, G. R. S. Mead . . .

All out of memory. Canto 74, like all *The Pisan Cantos*, is a
poem of memory, from a prodigious memory. But also, using
the word in the sense that William Carlos Williams gave it, it is a
poem of invention, a triumph of invention. So let me close with
the quotation that best expresses the nature and power of memory. This is from the third stanza of Cavalcanti's "Donna mi
pregha," in Pound's final version in Canto 36:

> In quella parte
> > dove sta memoria
> Prende suo stato
> > si formato
> > > chome
> Diafan dal lume
> > d'una schuritade
>
> La qual da Marte
> > viene e fá dimora
> Elgli é creato
> > e a sensato
> > > nome
> D'alma chostume
> > di chor volontade
>
> Where memory liveth,
> > it takes its state
> Formed like a diafan from light on shade
> Which shadow cometh of Mars and remaineth
> Created, having a name sensate,
> Custom of the soul,
> > will from the heart

POUND'S ECONOMICS

Time was when we could read the *Cantos* without worrying too much about Pound's economic theories. We could put them down to eccentricity. We could admire the splendor of the Usura Canto, the glorious language and the power of the rhythm, but skip over the monetary history in Cantos 96 and 97. We had to know something about his economics to understand the sorrows and, in his own word, the "errors" that Pound acknowledged in his last years. But we did not grasp, or at least I did not grasp, many of the implications of the ideas about money in the texture of the poem.

Such separation is no longer possible because of an astonishing but as yet unpublished paper, "The Economy of Poetry/The Poetry of Economics," by Richard Sieburth of New York University. After this paper, which applies semiotic, psychoanalytic, and Marxist methods of criticism to Pound's conceptions of monetary and poetic representation, we will never again be able to read the *Cantos* without seeing linguistic connections that we previously had not recognized.

Sieburth's analysis of the relationship between Pound's writings and his economic theories is so complex that I cannot possibly give a fair summary of it. But some of the main themes turn on poetry and naming and the minting of money. Sieburth deals with Pound's obsession with the stamp of sovereignty impressed on money and equally on poetry. He points out a pervasive duality, or "doubling." Usury is thus the excremental doppelgänger of *poetic* gold. Sieburth compares the "doubling" of poetry and economics in Pound's work to Freud's interpretation of the antithetical meaning of some primary words. "Sacred" usually means "holy" but can also mean "defiled"; "altus" is both "high" and "low." Sieburth "deconstructs" these reversibilities in Pound's work until we are almost ready to believe that his surname (£) predestined him to become a poet-economist, and that "Ezry/Usury" is more than a pun.

In his later years, as he moved toward silence, Pound wrote me of his worry that he could not make the *Cantos* "cohere." Sieburth suggests that Pound believed he could write the poem "on credit—the future tense of money," a loan which would be repaid in full when the "Paradiso" cantos eventually made the whole structure clear. But, to our sorrow, Pound's declining health did not permit the triumphant and revelatory closure. The last drafts and fragments are beautiful, but they are subdued and often melancholy. But the poem ends with the sturdy imperative: "To be men not destroyers." In this spirit Pound gave battle to the bankers.

Why Economics?

People often ask why Pound, whose education was in languages, literature, and history, thought he could become an economist. Quite simply, he identified with Odysseus and knew that he, E. P., was also *polumetis*, "a man of cunning and many skills." He could do anything. He made his own furniture and taught himself Chinese from dictionaries. He was slightly tone deaf and could play only with one finger on his clavichord, but he wrote two short operas which are still performed. He only failed as a sculptor. Brancusi gave him some small pieces of stone to cut but he chucked them in the *poubelle*.

I think we should dispose immediately of the myth that Pound became interested in monetary reform because his grandfather, Thaddeus Coleman Pound, not long after the Civil War, printed his own money for the use of the employees of his Union Lumbering Company in Chippewa Falls, Wisconsin.

Pound venerated Thaddeus—even more than he did the Loo-
mis brothers on his mother's side, who he told me were hanged
for stealing horses (though there is no documentation on the
hangings), but he admitted that he did not realize the full importance of Thaddeus's scrip until he had studied Silvio Gesell.
(One can read about Thaddeus, who appears as Thadeus Cuth-
bertson Weight, in Pound's *Indiscretions*, which can now be found
most easily in the collection called *Pavannes and Divagations*.)

Another explanation, which probably has more substance, is
that the death of Pound's great friend the sculptor Henri Gaudier-Brzeska in the First World War led to his concern with monetary reform. This proposition, and one hears it often, is based
on the fact that Pound was rocked by the death of Gaudier and
so many others. As he wrote in *Mauberley*:

> There died a myriad,
> And of the best, among them,
> For an old bitch gone in the teeth,
> For a botched civilization.

And earlier in the same sequence:

> Died some, pro patria,
>   non "dulce" non "et decor" . . .
> walked eye-deep in hell
> believing in old men's lies, then unbelieving
> came home, home to a lie,
> home to many deceits
> home to old lies and new infamy;
> usury age-old and age-thick . . .

Pound then set out to study the causes of war, concluding
that armament makers and bankers were as much responsible as
generals and politicians. Schneider-Creusot, he discovered, sold
cannons to both France and Germany. Looking into banking, he
learned that banks created money for loans *ex nihil*, simply by
book-entry, listing loans as a form of deposit. (The permitted

ratio of "loan deposits" to real deposits varies, but in this country today it can go as high as nine to one.)

> Said Paterson:
>> *Hath benefit of interest on all*
>> *the moneys which it, the bank, creates out of*
>> *nothing.*
>
> (CANTO 46)

So Pound was more than ripe for the theory of Social Credit when he met Major C. H. Douglas in A. R. Orage's office at the *New Age* in 1918.[1]

But from my conversations with him, I suspect that the Gaudier–Douglas chain was only a part of Pound's motivation. Consider his poverty during the years in London. He was the hot young poet around town but so poor that he often had to write to his father in Wyncote, "Dear Dad, Can you send me five dollars?" (There are a number of such appeals in the collection of letters to his parents that Mary de Rachewiltz is now editing.) Along with that penury was his confidence that he was on the way to becoming a great poet. Not surprisingly, he was convinced that the economic system should be so ordered as to provide a living for writers and artists. It did not do so because the banks controlled the system, making money scarce so they might lend it at high rates. Canto 45 centers chiefly on artists. But certainly the plight of poets was in Pound's mind long before that canto was written.

Social Credit and More

When we speak of Pound's economics we think of him first as a Social Crediter. His economics began with Social Credit but went far beyond this movement. I can't prove it, but Pound may have been the inventor, intellectually at least, of the Cuisinart. He kept pouring new ingredients into the ever-protesting gullet of Major Douglas. I'm not certain of the exact dates of the contaminations, but there followed Gesellism, with its stamp scrip

(Schwundgeld) and velocity of circulation; the attacks on usury by the canonists such as Saint Ambrose; his research into the history of the Monte dei Paschi bank in Siena; the history of coinage in the books of Alexander Del Mar; the structure of the Fascist corporations; the cullings from Jefferson, Adams, and Van Buren; the ideas of Confucius and Mencius on taxation; and borrowings from many contemporary writers: Brooks Adams, Montgomery Butchart, Irving Fisher, Christopher Hollis, Arthur Kitson, P. J. Larranaga, A. R. Orage, Willis Overholser, Odon Por, Frederick Soddy, Jerry Voorhis, McNair Wilson, W. E. Woodward, and others.

Pound even found a clue in the Latin translation of Aristotle's "nummum nummus non parit" (money does not beget money), a phrase that does not seem to have found its way into the *Cantos*, probably because he would have had to change it to "Nummum nummus parire non debet," (money *should not* beget money). However, he did manage to mistranslate Harry Stottle's *metathamenon* five times. "Harry Stottle" was what he always called the Stagirite in his letters to me.

By the time of the Second World War Pound's articles had become so heretical, such a potpourri, that the High-Church Douglasite magazines would no longer print them. He began sending them to me to agent for him in this country but I didn't have much luck. For some reason *Harper's* and the *Atlantic* were not enthusiastic. And in a letter of 1937 we find Pound asking H. L. Mencken: "Who the hell cares about Doug. schemes?" By then the disenchantment had become mutual.

C. H. Douglas

Clifford Hugh Douglas, the inventor of Social Credit, died in 1952 at the age of 73. He was a successful British engineer who worked for Westinghouse in India, for a railroad in Argentina, and for the London Post Office tube system. At some point he must have been in the army; he was always called "Major." Douglas's first book, *Economic Democracy*, which Orage helped him write, was serialized in the *New Age* in 1919. He went on to write nine more books, developing his themes and their implications for a better society. He was an ardent believer in democracy and no socialist. (Pound used to tell me that "Marx never understood money.") The fact that Douglas was able to get so many books published shows that his movement had considerable support in England, as well as in New Zealand and in the Canadian province of Alberta.

Douglas was not trained as an economist, but with an engineer's savvy for what made things work—and not work—he detected flaws in the world's economic system. He observed that in wartime there was an abundance of credit for armaments, but that in peacetime there was a shortage of credit for social uses, expanding businesses, and employment.

The American Social Credit party, of which I was a member while at Harvard, never got very far despite the handbills that I distributed in the cars of the Boston Mass Transit and the excellent magazine *New Democracy*, which the critic Gorham Munson edited in New York.

Douglas's books are not nearly so dry as most textbooks of economics, but they are hardly entertaining and now, with the increasing complexity of our system, they are not up to date. A selective bibliography will be found at the end of this book. Prophets are not necessarily their own best explainers. E. S. Holter did a primer called *Social Credit* (1934), but the most useful book is Gorham Munson's *Aladdin's Lamp* (1945), which covers the whole area of credit reform. Hugh Kenner, of course, has a stimulating chapter on Douglas in *The Pound Era*. And Earl Davis's *Vision Fugitive: Ezra Pound and Economics* (1968) is a comprehensive introduction.

As we look at Social Credit, I consider Douglas and Orage a team. Not only did Orage coach Douglas with his writing, and probably often rewrote him, he was the social philosopher of the doctrine. As Wendy Flory points out, "Orage supplied the visionary quality to the statistical basis of Social Credit." Orage's vision of "a more humane society" (which we must compare with Pound's dream of a *paradiso terrestre*) gave Social Credit much of its appeal. As Pound wrote in the *ABC of Economics*,

"Economics, as science, has no messianic call to alter the instincts." But a call was needed to get action.

The central proposition of Social Credit was Douglas's controversial contention that total costs exceed total purchasing power. (It is said that this revelation came to him when he was going over the accounts of the Royal Aircraft Works at Farnborough.) Douglas expressed this shortfall in his A+B theorem. A stands for income—principally salaries, wages, and dividends—which enter the economy as purchasing power. B represents plant and bank costs which, Douglas claimed, do not contribute to purchasing power. A will not purchase B, he said. No "reputable," orthodox economist has ever been known to endorse this A+B theorem. It is seen as an oversimplification because it does not take into account the timing and rates of flow of money movements. Pound, of course, dismissed these objections as part of the stupidity of the academics in the despised "beaneries," who were all under the thumb of the banks to keep their jobs. And he explained to me that Threadneedle Street (the Bank of England) had ordered Fleet Street (the London press) never to print Douglas's name, so that, when Douglas was invited to the queen's garden party at Buckingham Palace, his name was missing from the guest list.

Douglas's proposal for increasing purchasing power to meet the A+B shortfall was the National Dividend, an interesting variant on Keynes and perhaps an early form of monetarism. All citizens, except those whose income was four times the amount of the dividend, would go to the post office to collect their dividend, for which they need do no work, because they were entitled to it as a child of the sun, from which comes the energy that makes the world productive. This rationale, at least, was provided me by John Hargrave, the leader of the British Social Credit party. The amount of the dividend would fluctuate periodically, being calibrated to the rates of production and consumption. A National Monetary Authority would do the computations. These infusions would raise purchasing power above costs and so increase employment.

Orage and Douglas shrewdly foresaw that technology and

robotics would reduce jobs. They conceived that the time would come when there could not be full employment and the National Dividend would sustain those who had no work. Today welfare and unemployment insurance furnish this protection at great cost to the taxpayer. The source of funds for the dividends would be the same as what is now used for monetary expansion —book entry, but on the books of the state, not the banks. It would be *social* credit, based on the productive capacity of the nation and the ability of its people to exploit their skills and "the abundance of nature."

What is this flam-flam—just more printing press money? To understand we must try to put ourselves in the minds of the Social Crediters and forget all traditional principles of economics. Social Credit rejects the gold standard and the idea that money is a limited commodity. Pound always said that money was simply a ticket to get goods and services from one place to another. The purpose of money was to distribute abundance to everyone. "You don't need kilometers," he said, "to build a road."

You can imagine, I'm sure, the indignation that the idea of a National Dividend provoked. The poor protested that, despite the exclusions, the middle classes had no right to it, and the rich complained that the lower classes were mostly shiftless and already on the dole. Less prejudiced individuals suggested that so much new money would lead to inflation. Douglas's answer was a mechanism he called the Just Price. This was to be a retail discount that would peg selling prices to the real cost of production, exclusive of *financial* costs. Like the dividend, the discount would fluctuate to achieve the right balance between inflation and deflation. It represents price control, such as many nations have used in wartime.

Pound's belief in the Just Price was confirmed when he turned up a similar concept in his study of some of the canonists in Migne, though with them, I think, the interest was more on Christian morality than in turning the economic wheels.

To me the appeal of the National Dividend is that it would inject new money—and new money is apparently necessary for an expanding economy—throughout the social pyramid so that it would work its way up to those at the top who, as we all know, most deserve it, but would give much comfort to those less smart or industrious in the process. As things are now—if I understand the current system correctly—an increase in the money supply is ordained by the Federal Reserve but is put out through the banks, who use a fair part of it to finance such worthy causes as the takeovers of one huge corporation by another, loans to Latin America which will never be repaid, star wars factories—but who do not loan much money to the needy residents of Newark and Bedford-Stuyvesant.

Silvio Gesell's Stamp Scrip

Silvio Gesell was not a famous economist; Pound tells us in Canto 74 that he was minister of finance for "rather less than five days" in the Lindhauer socialist government of Bavaria following the First World War. Gesell was a German who had made a fortune in Argentina and began to think about the nature and flow of money. His invention was *Schwundgeld*, or stamp scrip, a self-liquidating currency that would discourage hoarding and increase the velocity of circulation. This money was a measure of work. The legend on my ten-schilling note from Wörgl, Austria, is interesting. It reads: "Nothilfe Wörgl/ Bestätigter Arbeitswerk," "Wörgl help in emergency/Confirmed value of work."

"Schwund" means "dwindling." *Schwundgeld* was a bill with squares on the back on which the bearer periodically had to place a postage stamp to keep it valid. A fully stamped note would be replaced at the bank by a new one. Details of the system appear in Gesell's book, *The New Economic Order*. It is subtitled "A plan to secure an uninterrupted exchange of the products of labor, free from bureaucratic interference, usury and exploitation."

Stamp scrip, as Pound pointed out, put a tax on money itself, but one that would be paid by those who could afford it. Is there some comparison with Henry George's Single Tax, which would

Pound and Laughlin during lunch stop on drive over the mountains to Austria.

have taxed only land, not income? Like Confucius and Mencius, Pound disapproved of unfair taxation, which was probably the primary appeal for him of Gesell's theory. Gesell also opposed unearned income such as interest and rents. The references to Gesell are in Canto 41, page 205; Canto 74, pages 441–2, and Canto 80, page 507.

So far as I know Gesell's Schwundgeld was only tried out, and on a strictly local basis, in two communities: Wörgl and Schwanenkirchen in Austria. One of my most interesting trips with Ezra and Olga was driving them from Venice up to Gais to see their daughter Mary and then over the Brenner to visit Herr Unterguggenberger, the deposed mayor of Wörgl. Wörgl is a pleasant town of about six thousand on the River Inn in the mountains of the Tyrol. It was usually a rather prosperous town, being a junction point on the railroad between Munich, the Brenner, and Vienna, with lumbering from the mountains and good farms in the valley bottoms. But the depression hit it hard, and no money was circulating. Unterguggenberger had heard of

Schwundgeld and printed some for the town. Pound tells about the Wörgl experiment on page 314 of the *Selected Prose,* how Schwundgeld restored prosperity for three years until "all the lice of Europe, Rothschildian and otherwise" found out about it and had the central bank in Vienna crack down on Wörgl. Or as he presents it in Canto 74:

> the state need not borrow
> as was shown by the mayor of Wörgl
> who had a milk route
> and whose wife sold shirts and short breeches
> and on whose book-shelf was the Life of Henry Ford
> and also a copy of the Divina Commedia
> and of the Gedichte of Heine
> a nice little town in the Tyrol in a wide flat-lying valley
> near Innsbruck and when a note of the
> small town of Wörgl went over
> a counter in Innsbruck
> and the banker saw it go over
> all the slobs in Europe were terrified
> "no one" said the Frau Burgomeister
> "in this village who cd/ write a newspaper article.
> Knew it was money but pretended it was not
> in order to be on the safe side of the law."

I know how much Gesellism meant to Pound from a letter he wrote me in 1970—one of the last letters I had from him. He was still worrying about stamp scrip. He said: "Stamp scrip is impractical as, even when the bills were printed on really good paper, they wore out and went back to treasury to be pulped at end of six months. Also the bother of looking at each separate note to see if it was properly stamped. This does not exclude the use of local money in an emergency..."

Del Mar

Alexander Del Mar was another of Pound's great enthusiasms. Periodically he urged me to reprint one of Del Mar's books, but I never got interested. Del Mar (1836–1926), like Douglas, was an engineer, though chiefly in mining. His avocations were the study of precious metals, the history of coinage, and monetary systems. He published some thirty books with such titles as *Money and Civilization* and *Roman and Moslem Moneys*. But the one that appealed most to Pound was Del Mar's *History of Monetary Crimes*, which explored the sovereignty of money and how good rulers throughout history had controlled, and bad ones manipulated, first coinage and later currency and credit. Del Mar believed that a high civilization required an exclusive system of money issued and guaranteed by the state. This view ties in with Pound's repeated insistence that the Constitution gave Congress the sole right to issue money, a right which was taken over by the banks, a capture which the resistance of Adams and Jefferson, Jackson, Van Buren, and Lincoln could not reverse.

> The Congress shall have power; to coin money
> regulate the value thereof and of foreign coin
> and to fix the standard of weights and measures.
>
> (*Constitution of the U.S. Article I*
> *Legislative Department, Section 8, page 5.*)

There are sprinklings from Del Mar's books on coinage in Cantos 89, 96, and 97.

Usury

> Usura rusteth the chisel
> It rusteth the craft and the craftsman.
>
> (CANTO 45)

Usury, of course, is a major element in Pound's economics. Douglas and Orage, however, did not often use the term in

Ezra's sense of it. They were more likely to speak of "bank charges." Pound's sense of usury came, I think, from the canonist writers, principally Saint Ambrose. At the end of Canto 45 Pound defined usury:

> N.B. Usury: A charge for the use of purchasing power, levied without regard to production; often without regard to the possibilities of production. (Hence the failure of the Medici bank.)

This position is Social Credit doctrine, of course, but in Pound's mind it was also tied to Ambrose and the Monte dei Paschi bank of Siena.

The linking phrase is Ambrose's "captans annonam maledictus in plebe sit," (may seizing the harvest be [considered] a curse on the people) which Professor Wilhelm has located in Ambrose's *De Tobia* (*Patrologia Latina*, Volume 14), a commentary on the apocryphal *Book of Tobias*. Pound translated "captans annonam" as "hoggers of the harvest." The *De Tobia* attacked Jewish usurers who ruined farmers with high rates of interest on crop loans. (Duke Leopold of Siena was one of Pound's heroes because he limited the Monte dei Paschi to 3 percent on loans to the peasants.) Pound had nothing against bank loans that supported any kind of production at a fair rate. And he had nothing against service banking. In fact, all his life he had a savings account at a bank in Jenkintown, Pennsylvania.

Fascism

Fascism was part of Pound's economics because of the corporations, which were rather like guilds. These were Mussolini's replacement for labor unions. The corporations, Pound told me, would make an ideal social basis for the implementation of Social Credit. Although Pound was working on his *Jefferson and/or Mussolini* in 1934, he did not give me much detail about the corporations. The "Jeff/Muss," as he always called the book, is extremely discursive, but it does have a central theme: that the Jeffersonian political tradition had been reborn, not in Virginia,

Pound at the Golden Rose Inn in Salzburg, 1935.

but in Mussolini's Italy. From this brief summary, I dare say, you can tell whether you want to read it.

When I was studying at the Ezuversity I tried to learn some Italian. Pound gave me a collection of Mussolini's *Scritti e Discorsi* as an example of "clean and clear" Italian prose. That it was—very declarative—but did Mussolini write it himself? It was a great day in Rapallo when Il Duce passed through the town giving *darshan* to the populace. We watched from a balcony. No need for security guards as everyone loved him. He came down the *fronte* standing in an open car, giving the salute, or blessing. He was a bit chubby, but he knew about eye contact; at least six people told me that he had smiled directly at them.

Public and Private Debt

Should we take Pound's economic theories seriously? Certainly we must be aware of them to understand the *Cantos* and his life. But do they have any practical application for the muddle we are in today? I think that Pound had cracker-barrel horse sense about the pyramiding of debt, both public and private. And I think Douglas and Orage were right in trying to make credit rather than debt the basis of the economy. I'm sure you've seen those pie-shaped charts that show where the U.S. taxpayers' money is going. The last one I looked at showed over 30 percent going to service the national debt. I grant that much government interest provides income which is spent. Yet much of the national debt—I don't know the figures—is held by banks.

Private debt is astronomical. Again, dividends and interest contribute to spendable income. But what about the takeovers among giant industries? DuPont eats Conoco. SoCal swallows Gulf. The acquiring companies accomplish these engorgements through loans given by banks at high interest. Then for decades the acquiring companies will use their profits to pay back the loans and the interest. Stockholders will suffer. Mergers usually increase unemployment when staffs are consolidated. This is bank capitalism at its worst. A dozen investment banking firms are scouting these deals for industrial companies. Is this the right way to use credit—which is fundamentally based on the people's faith in their government—for productive purposes?

The book *Funny Money* by Marc Singer, a *New Yorker* reporter, would delight Pound. It's an eye-opener on how banks can get away with murder—up to a point. It documents how some young bankers in Oklahoma City used Paterson's principle of creating book-entry money *ex nihil* to make high interest loans to gas drillers, and what befell them all. The little Penn Square bank nearly bankrupted the great Continental Illinois Bank of Chicago by selling it some of the bad loans. I understand that to date Washington has had to pour nearly seven billion dollars of the taxpayers' money into saving Continental Illinois to prevent a domino-effect collapse of other major money-center banks.

Many banking practices beyond the creation of money *ex nihil* are concealed from the public. But one surfaced in the *New York Times* business section on June 24, 1985, under the heading "Worrisome Bank Obligations." The Federal bank regulators apparently do not require banks to include on their balance sheets loan guarantees or commitments to make loans, though the banks collect fees from them. The *Times* reporter estimated the value of these hidden instruments at over a trillion dollars. Paterson didn't do that well. Most people are unaware, as Alfred Kazin has pointed out, of the present campaign by the banks to tamper with anti-usury regulations so that they may manipulate their rates on credit card interest. Delinquent credit card balances keep soaring as the banks promote more cards to the public. It's a house of cards headed for collapse.

Pound's wit makes the style of many of his economic writings diverting, but one sequence is really comical—the verses which he did for *The New English Weekly* as "Alfie Venison, the poet of Titchfield Street." These poems are reprinted as Appendix II of *Personae*, and include:

SONG OF SIX HUNDRED M.P.'S

> We are 'ere met together
> in this momentous hower,
> Ter lick th' bankers' dirty boots
> an' keep the Bank in power.

> We are 'ere met together
> ter grind the same old axes
> And keep the people in its place
> a' payin' us the taxes.

> We are six hundred beefy men
> (but mostly gas and suet)
> An' every year we meet to let
> some other feller do it.

Pound's economic theories were a mishmash of eccentricities. But they were inspired by his millenial optimism and his assurance that he knew the answers. He wanted to create the *paradiso terrestre* of a just economic system without resorting to socialism or revolution. The *Cantos* themselves with their revisions of history and their citation of honest men of the past — Adams and Jefferson, certain Chinese emperors, Duke Leopold and others — were part of the process. (In Canto 71, Adams tells us that "every bank of discount is downright corruption.") But Pound's dream may never come true except in his own imaginary cities — Wagadu, "4 times rebuilded," and Dioce, "whose terraces are the colour of stars."

In Herodotus's account, the city of Dioce had its battlements plated with silver and gold. Why did Pound turn silver and gold into the "colour of stars"? Was it because "colour of stars" is so beautiful, as image and as language, or because, without realizing it, he did not wish to signify the sovereignty of money in his sacred city?

Postscript: Lewis Hyde on Pound

When I prepared this paper I had not read the revelatory chapter on Pound's economic and political ideas in Lewis Hyde's book *The Gift*. Had I done so, much of my focus would have been different, more theoretical and relating Pound's thought to concepts in a broader cultural range. I don't want to degrade the originality and subtlety of Hyde's interpretations by a bad paraphrase so I will simply urge the reader to turn to *The Gift*, which is published by Vintage.

E.P.

THE LIGHTER SIDE

It often surprises me when I read the many books about Pound and the essays in the journals, how little attention is given to his humor. The only specialized piece on the subject which I have encountered is Michael Alexander's "Pound's Sense of Humour" in the Pound issue of *Agenda* in 1980. What explains this lack of interest in Pound's wit? Is it that the scholar-critics don't think it important, or is it because, most of them not having known him, they never had the opportunity to learn from his conversation how central humor was to him as a writer and as a critic? Humor was part of the fabric of his mind, and, inevitably, it went into his work.

I had the privilege of knowing Pound rather well. After I studied with him in his Ezuversity in Rapallo in 1935, I became his publisher in 1938, and am still bringing out volumes of his correspondence. Over the years he wrote me about five hundred letters, wonderfully instructive letters in which wisdom was salted with wit. In his prime he was the best, the funniest talker I ever knew. Our classes at the Ezuversity took place mostly at the lunch table and I have never had such entertainment. He practiced what I believe the rhetoricians call tapinosis, the application of colorful slang to serious topics, and we were given Villon and the troubadours, or even Dante, in his vernacular.

I'd like to suggest that the comic, with Pound, was more than a personality trait. It was so instinctive that it became a considerable element in his method of composition, both in prose and in poetry. If this was true, was it intentional? Or did the humor simply come out of itself, a product of his ebullience?

Word Play

The congruence of wit and wisdom is most visible in his letters, those extraordinarily visual pages in which it was quite clear that he was trying to destroy his typewriter, something I saw in Rapallo when his pounding and slashing at the space bar made his whole desk shake. And the word play! More tapinosis. New Directions to the embarrassment of the Norfolk postmistress became Nude Erections. "The embalsamation of the late Rabbit Britches" referred to Robert Bridges, who wrote "Worse Libre" in one of his "leetle bookies." "Licherchoor and deh Awta of the Hoccydent." "Wot he finks a styge (notta Stooge) play orter be . . . lanwige of Agon suatained thru a lively and brefftakink ax-shun to a Tomthunderink KlimuXX." "Pasqual meddertashuns" was Easter duty. "Greek flylozzerfers in the Low*ebb* Classics."

Michael Alexander is very good on Pound's interlingual puns, including a few with Chinese words, and on the range of logo-daedaly in the *Cantos*. In Canto 94 we find:

and Apollonius said to King Huey

梁 Leang

惠 Hwuy

The top character is the name of the Liang dynasty. The one below it is that of King Hui, one of the "good" Chinese rulers, that is, one whose economic practices were sound. The seven ideograms that follow tell of "Hui of Liang, by wealth put to use not by wealth hoarded." So Hui of Liang becomes Huey Long, who, I've heard, built miles of highways in Louisiana and was most generous to its university.

The use of the comic, as a rhetorical device, appears in many of the prose books, particularly in such pieces in *Pavannes and*

Divagations, as *Indiscretions*, where the humor is ironic, and in the *ABC of Reading*, but even more in *Kulchur*, where Pound let himself go with some vim. And elsewhere, as in the 1964 foreword to the reprint of *A Lume Spento*, which he called "a collection of stale cream puffs—chocolate creams who hath forgotten you?"

The "Giessen Roll"

It is in the poems of *Personae* that Pound's humor matures. When he began writing he was so in love with the nineteenth century—with the Pre-Raphaelites, Browning, and Swinburne —that there was small possibility of indulging his comic sense. But by 1911 a landmark event in modern poetry had taken place, the "Giessen roll," when Ford Madox Ford convinced Pound (they were in Giessen) that his stilted Edwardian language wouldn't do. To show his concern, Ford rolled on the floor. Pound then set out to clean up his idiom.

Pound published *Marvoil*, which is his mask of the troubadour Arnaut de Mareuil, in 1909 in his third book. This is not a funny poem—Arnaut had a disappointing life: he lost his lady and was booted out of the castle—yet Pound tells the story with a slightly comic intonation, a tone which will recur in some of the mini-masks of the *Cantos*. (Compare the tone of *Marvoil* with that of *Piere Vidal Old*.) In *Marvoil*, I believe, we find the first major pun in his verse, where he refers to the "poke-nose" Alfonso of Aragon as "half-bald," a locution which escaped the notice of the London printers.

In 1913, Pound wrote to Harriet Monroe, ". . . good art thrives in an atmosphere of parody. Parody is, I suppose, the best criticism—it sifts the durable from the apparent." In 1911, in *Canzoni*, colloquial parody makes its appearance in "Mr. Housman's Message":

> O woe, woe,
> People are born and die,
> We also shall be dead pretty soon

Therefore let us act as if we were
        dead already.

The bird sits on the hawthorn tree
But he dies also, presently.
Some lads get hung, and some get shot.
Woeful is this human lot.
        Woe! woe, etcetera....

London is a woeful place,
Shropshire is much pleasanter.
Then let us smile a little space
Upon fond nature's morbid grace.
        Oh, Woe, woe, woe, etcetera....

A Kind of Deflationary Mockery

In the same year and book, there is another new tone — one that
I find hard to label. It is in "Au Salon," which was originally
part of the "Und Drang" sequence. It is a tone that will be developed in the *Homage to Sextus Propertius* and be used frequently in
the *Cantos*. Call it perhaps a kind of deflationary mockery. It isn't
precisely satire, but it sounds like put-down. The poet knows
better than his characters and is telling them so.

I suppose, when poetry comes down to facts,
When our souls are returned to the gods
        And the spheres they belong in,
Here in the every-day where our acts
Rise up and judge us;

I suppose there are a few dozen verities
That no shift of mood can shake from us:

One place where we'd rather have tea
(Thus far hath modernity brought us)
"Tea" (Damn you!)

Have tea, damn the Caesars,
Talk of the latest success, give wind to some scandal,
Garble a name we detest, and for prejudice?
Set loose the whole consummate pack
    to bay like Sir Roger de Coverley's

This our reward for our works,
    sic crescit gloria mundi:
Some circle of not more than three
    that we prefer to play up to,
Some few whom we'd rather please
    than hear the whole aegrum vulgus
Splitting its beery jowl
    a-meaowling our praises.

Some certain peculiar things,
    cari laresque, penates,
Some certain accustomed forms,
    the absolute unimportant.

There is a variation of this tone in the seven-page verse cause-
rie, "Redondillas, or Something of that Sort," which, as I have
previously mentioned, Pound cut from the proofs of *Canzoni*,
though he allowed me to publish it in a limited edition in 1967.
But here he has worked out a rather formal metric structure of
false parallels or comic antithesis which he did not pursue further.

I believe in some lasting sap
    at work in the trunk of things;
I believe in a love of deeds,
    in a healthy desire for action;
I believe in double-edged thought
    in careless destruction.

I believe in some parts of Nietzsche,
    I prefer to read him in sections;
In my heart of hearts I suspect him

of being the one modern christian;
Take notice I never have read him
            except in English selections.

I am sick of the toothless decay
            of God's word as they usually preach it;
I am sick of bad blasphemous verse
            that they sell with their carols and hymn tunes. . . .

In the following years he gave us such humorous gems as
"The New Cake of Soap," "The Bath Tub," and this from
"Meditatio":

When I carefully consider the curious habits of dogs
I am compelled to conclude
That man is the superior animal.

When I consider the curious habits of man
I confess, my friend, I am puzzled.

and "Ancient Music":

Winter is icummen in,
Lhude sing Goddamm,
Raineth drop and staineth slop,
And how the wind doth ramm! . . .

and "Cantico del Sole":

The thought of what America would be like
If the Classics had a wide circulation
            Troubles my sleep
The thought of what America,
The thought of what America,
The thought of what America would be like
If the Classics had a wide circulation
            Troubles my sleep

Nunc demittis, now lettest thou thy servant,
Now lettest thou thy servant
    Depart in peace."

In *Mauberley*, "Mr. Nixon," who was probably Arnold Bennett, is a mix of humor and satire. This is the kind of story with which Pound enthralled the students at the Ezuversity. Its bantering tone often reappears in the *Cantos*. Pound said that "the way of the ironical is beset with snares and furze-bushes," but he did not hesitate to echo Laforgue's irony in *Mauberley*.

A Literary Hoax

Speaking of *Mauberley*, the story of its genesis as a hoax is perhaps relevant. One convivial evening in London, Pound and Eliot decided that it would be amusing to invent an impossible poet who would write parodies of poets they didn't like and lampooning reviews of such poets' books. Hugh Selwyn Mauberley was the name they dreamed up. A friend spilled the beans on that plan so they hatched up another—my informant on this was Basil Bunting—to write a hoax in emulation of Samuel Butler III, that droll fellow who tried to prove that the *Odyssey* was written by a woman. This scheme also collapsed and *Mauberley* became a serious poem, one of Pound's most important masks. It will be a major event when Valerie Eliot releases the Old Possum/Br'er Rabbit correspondence. I once read some of those exchanges and I'm still laughing.

S.P. & E.P.

The *Homage to Sextus Propertius* was one of Pound's favorites. When I asked him what text he would like to have handprinted by Giovanni Mardersteig of Verona, he chose the *Propertius* and *Mauberley*, giving the combination the title of *Diptych*. The *Propertius* may be the best of his masks—the longest and the most richly conceived, the most complete identification with an earlier poet. Part of that richness is its humor. First the play of anachronism: "nor is it [my cellar] equipped with a frigidaire patent."

The lampooning of the Augustan Establishment stands, of course, for Pound's contempt for our own establishments:

> Annalists will continue to record Roman reputations,
> Celebrities from the Trans-Caucasus will belaud
>> Roman
>>> celebrities
> And expound the distentions of Empire.

And Pound's ascription to Propertius of a "bit of humor and irony which the dessicated do not see" speaks for his own wit, as in such lines as:

> the devirginated young ladies...

> And if she plays with me with her shirt off,
>> We shall construct many Iliads.

> And my ventricles do not palpitate to Caesarial *ore rotundos,*

> It is noble to die of love, and honorable to remain
>> uncuckolded for a season.

> "You are a very early inspector of mistresses."

> Zeus' clever rapes, in the old days

> Of all these young women
>> not one has enquired the cause of the world...

I don't recall that Pound ever mentioned the Latin poet Persius, but the other day I happened to be reading Persius's first satire, which is an attack on the corruption of literary taste in Rome, and suddenly it sounded to me like parts of the *Propertius,* even in G. G. Ramsay's rather ponderous translation:

We write something grand that will take a vast amount of breath
to pant out. This stuff you will someday read aloud to the public,
having first lubricated your throat with an emollient wash...

An Ear for Accents

In assessing Pound's humor we should not overlook his passion
for accents and dialects. He had an incredible ear. In his mono-
logues he loved to tell stories in dialect. He had a number of
them, many of which turn up in the *Cantos*.

There is the American Black accent, which we hear in the
voices of the prisoners in the Pisan camp. I think this accent took
root when Pound as a child read Joel Chandler Harris's "Uncle
Remus" stories, which he later read to his own grandchildren at
Brunnenburg. And this, of course, is the origin of "Old Possum" and "Br'er Rabbit" in the Pound/Eliot friendship.

Then there was the "Oirrish" accent, used most notably in
Canto 83, the lines about Yeats:

> as it were the wind in the chimney
> > but was in reality Uncle William
> downstairs composing
> that had made a great Peeeeacock
> > in the proide ov his oiye
>
> . . . .
>
> made a great peacock
> > in the proide of his oyyee.

I'm not sure that this accent began with Uncle Willie Yeats at
the Stone Cottage in Sussex in 1913. Perhaps it started with
Finley Peter Dunne's "Mr. Dooley."

> Well, said Mr Dooley, 'at th' age whin a boy is fit to be in colledge I
> wudden't have him around th' house.

I know how Pound loved the Oirrish accent because when,
after he was released from St. Elizabeths, I coaxed him to go to a

recording studio, he was terribly nervous until he got into his Celtic, keening chant, as you hear it on the Caedmon records. Then he enjoyed himself so much I could hardly get him to stop.

Perhaps the most famous accent is the American cracker-barrel of the hillbilly general store. This we hear in Canto 19:

> so I sez:
> Waal haow is it you're over here, right off the Champz Elyza?
> And how can yew be here? Why don't the fellers at home
> Take it all off you?...
> "Oh," he sez, ..."It's a long time since I ain't had tew
> rent any money."

There was a cockney accent, a Yiddish accent, a middle-European one, an Arab one, and even a lower-class French one as in Canto 16. All these voices were in Pound's head and are part of his humor.

There are some nice touches of humor in Pound's translations of the *Confucian Odes*:

> Yaller bird, let my corn alone,
> Yaller bird, let my crawps alone,
> These folks here won't let me eat,
> I wanna go back whaar I can meet
> the folks I used to know at home,
>   I got a home an' I wanna' git goin',...
>   "Huang Niao"

> State
> all a wobble,
> scanners and boobs—
> a few left to gobble—
> bright boys and planners,
> some who'll 'take trouble'
> all of a bubble
> down into quick-sand....
>   "Planners Raw Deal"

Flies, blue flies on a fence rail,
should a prince swallow lies wholesale? . . .

Guests start eatin', mild and even,
The sober sit an' keep behavin',
But say they've boozed when they do not.
When they've booz'd they start a-wavin' an' a-ravin', . . .

Equally important as a form of humor in the *Odes* is Pound's use of parody. If he detected in a Chinese text something that reminded him of a favorite English poem he often parodied its tone or stanzaic form in his translation. This produces some lovely echoes. To track them down should keep a graduate student happily occupied for most of a term.

Because of the collage structure, it is difficult to set out all the types of wit and humor in the *Cantos*. The mask technique has become the mini-mask to establish a character in a few lines, though Kung is fully developed in Canto 13, and in Canto 12 we have Baldy Bacon and John Quinn's classic story of the "pore honest sailor."

Doggerel

It's obvious from their gusto that Pound enjoyed himself with his doggerel verses. When he decided that he must "eggerkate" the British masses about Social Credit in what he supposed was their own lingo he chose the voice of "Alfie Venison, the Poet of Titchfield Street."

THE CHARGE OF THE
BREAD BRIGADE

Half a loaf, half a loaf,
Half a loaf? Um-hum?
Down through the vale of gloom
Slouched the ten million,
Onward th' 'ungry blokes,

Crackin' their smutty jokes!
We'll send 'em mouchin' 'ome,
Damn the ten million!

There goes the night brigade,
They got no steady trade,
Several old so'jers know
     Monty has blunder'd.
Theirs not to reason why,
Theirs but to buy the pie,
Slouching and mouching,
     Lousy ten million!

Plenty to right of 'em,
Plenty to left of 'em,
     Yes, wot is left of 'em,
Damn the ten million.
Stormed at by press and all,
How shall we dress 'em all?
     Glooming and mouching!

See 'em go slouching there,
With cowed and crouching air
     Dundering dullards!
How the whole nation shook
While Milord Beaverbrook
     Fed 'em with hogwash!

In the section of *Pavannes and Divagations* that Pound headed
"Frivolities," there are some nice comic verses such as "Mon-
sieur Pom-Pom allait en guerre/ per vendere cannoni"; the one
to King George V if the poet were chained to the fountain at
Buckingham Palace, "Oh bury 'er down in Blooms-buree/
where the gravy tastes like the soup"; the one about the "Tahai-
tian" princess and the poet; and the one to "Bill Yeats, the poet
twoice the soize of William Shakespear."

In Louis Zukofsky's *Objectivist Anthology* of 1932 we find the notorious "Yiddisher Charleston Band," which Pound sang to Dr. Kavka in St. Elizabeths. It begins:

> Gentle Jheezus sleek and wild
> Found disciples tall an' hairy
> Flirting with his red hot Mary,
>   Now hot momma Magdalene
>   Is doing front page fer the screen...

and includes an amical pick-up from one of Eliot's famous works:

> Ole king Bolo's big black queen
> Whose bum was big as a soup tureen...

Many of the funniest of the doggerel poems have not yet been collected because they were incorporated in letters to friends. Here is a fine ballad that he sent to Joyce in 1923:

> "Ballade of the most gallant Mulligan, Senator[1] in ordinary
>   and the frivolous milkwench of Hogan
>   afftl. dedicated to
>   S. Daedalus
>   Tenor
>   by his friend
>   Simm McNulty

> Ohe, ohe, Jock Hielandman,
> The strong and brawny Mulligan
> Took off his overcoat and ran
>   Unto the river Liffey,

> Peeled off his breeches and jumped in,
> Humecting thus his hairy skin;
> All heedless of pursuers' din
>   He struck out like a porpoise.

"Who goes there, where the waters pour
"Across the mill-dam, say, koind sir?"
"I am a celtic senator,"
        To her replied Buck Mulligan.

"Put on your breeches, sir, again,"
To him replied the milk-maiden,
"before you land by our hog-pen,
        on this side of the Liffey."

"Ach, darlint, do not but lend me yours,
"Oi left moine wid them rebel boors
"whom you see fearin' wather-cures
        on to'ther side the Liffey."

"Oi will, sir," says she, as cute a cheeze,
"To shield you from the gaelic breeze,
"Bedad, oi think they'll reach your knees,
        "Kind, kindly kind, sir senator,

"And I but one condition make
"Before I doff now for your sake
"—think—Jaysus! think what oi've at stake
        "O kindly kind, sir senator,

"If you will wear them and go down
"To the senate hall in Dublin Town
"In that attire,—do not frown,
"Promise me, dear; or, damn you, drown."

And here are two little jingles for "Old Possum" in letters to
Eliot:

SONG FER THE MUSES' GARDEN

Ez Po and Possum
Have picked all the blossom,

Let all the others
Run back to their mothers
    Fer a boye's bes' friend iz his Oedipus,
    A boy's best friend is his Oedipus.

Sez the Maltese dawg to the Siam cat
"Whaaar'z old Parson Possum at?"
Sez the Siam cat to the Maltese dawg
"Dahr he sets lak a bump-onna-log."

There was a world of marvelous fun in Ezra, it bubbled out of him, yet I submit that there was always considerable wisdom in his wit. In Canto 83 Pound cites Erigena's *hilaritas* as a virtue.

I'd like to leave you with a paradigm. Most of you will have heard about the photograph that caused such an uproar, the one showing Pound making the Fascist salute when he landed in Italy on his return from St. Elizabeths. It's not exactly what it seems. If you examine the picture with a magnifying glass you may detect that Pound is smiling, probably laughing at his own joke.

EZ AS WUZ

1. Henry Seidel Canby (1878–1961) taught at Yale for over twenty years. While he was an editor of the *Saturday Review of Literature,* he wrote a famous essay proving that there was no character development in Joyce's *Ulysses.*

2. A thorough analysis is Barry Goldensohn's "Pound and Anti-Semitism" in *The Yale Review,* Spring, 1986.

3. Bernard Baruch (1870–1965) was a famous Wall Street speculator. Before he reached the age of thirty, he had made his fortune on the stock market. He was well known in the federal government and was a national advisor on defense during World War I. He used to sit on a park bench in Washington and presidents would come out to get his advice. To Ezra he was a symbol of the Jewish banker—a "notorious financier."

4. Christian Herter (1895–1966) was the Secretary of State for President Dwight D. Eisenhower from 1959–61.

5. Mary is Ezra's daughter by Olga Rudge; she later became Princess Mary de Rachewiltz.

6. More information on the Eleusinian Mysteries is given in "Motz el Son."

POUND'S PEDAGOGY

1. The Dadaists were European anti-bourgeois experimental writers and artists of 1916–21. The movement was started by Tristan Tzara in Zurich. It stressed absurdity and the unexpected in artistic expression. The French movement, centering around André Breton, Louis Aragon, Man Ray, Jean Arp, and Marcel Duchamp, later merged into Surrealism.

2. The original edition of *Indiscretions* is very rare. The text will now be found in the *Pavannes and Divagations* collection.

3. In Pound's time various literary groups put out manifestoes which are important in the history of modern literature. See Marjorie Perloff: *The Futurist*

Moment: Avant-Garde, Avant-Guerre, and the Language of Rupture (University of Chicago Press, 1986). See chapter 3 for a definition and history of the manifesto and a discussion of Italian exemplars. Chapter 4 takes up some of the comparable Russian Futurist manifestoes. The Pound chapter (5) alludes to the *Blast* manifestoes and to Pound's own manifesto practice.

4. Arthur Waley (1889–1966) was a prolific British translator of Chinese literary texts, including *The Tale of Genji*, *The Nō Plays of Japan*, and *The Poetry and Career of Li Po*.

WALKING AROUND A WATER-BUTT

1. The best discussion of the Pound/Browning connection is George Bornstein's essay "Pound's Parlayings with Robert Browning" in the symposium *Ezra Pound among the Poets* (University of Chicago Press, 1985).

2. It's difficult to be sure who started calling them the Ur-Cantos but all Poundians call them that now. They were the drafts he published in *Poetry* magazine and in his 1919 book *Quia Pauper Amavi*. *Ur* is German for primitive. There is an *Ur-Faust* and also an *Ur-Hamlet*.

3. Booth Tarkington (1869–1946) and Sir Gilbert Parker (1862–1932) were both popular writers around the turn of the century. Tarkington was an American novelist who featured Midwest town life in such books as *The Magnificent Ambersons*, which won a Pulitzer Prize in 1918, and *Alice Adams*, which won a Pulitzer Prize in 1921. He also wrote the adolescent classics, *Seventeen* and *Penrod*. Parker was a Canadian historical novelist. He moved to England in 1889 and served in Parliament from 1900 to 1918. His novels include *Pierre and His People* and *The Promised Land*.

4. "The obese but meritorious F." is Ford Madox Ford.

5. "Whale" was Eliot's colleague F. V. Morley at Faber & Faber. Djuna Barnes (1892–1982) is best known for her novel *Nightwood*, which Eliot is said to have helped her organize.

6. Anthony Eden (1897–1977) entered Parliament in 1923. He was Prime Minister of Great Britain from 1955 to 1957.

MOTZ EL SON

1. "Alba Belingalis" was in the little London *Personae* of 1909. Pound did not include it in the big *Personae* collection. It is now on page 91 of *Collected Early Poems of Ezra Pound*, New Directions, 1976.

2. Pound's translation of Ventadorn's "The Lark" is on page 42 of *The Translations of Ezra Pound*. His translation of Rudel's "Amor de Lohn" is in the *Forked Branches* limited edition.

3. In the early version, page 135 of *The Translations of Ezra Pound*, Pound has it: "In memory's locus taketh he his state." But in the final version, which is in Canto 26, page 179, this becomes: "Where memory liveth, it takes its state."

4. Jongleur is another word for a minstrel. Most of them were player-singers who performed the poems of noble troubadours. But Roubaud says some wrote their own songs. I used "jongleur" here thinking of the instruments they may have used.

5. Pitkethly wrote the script for the documentary and I was a consultant. He produced and directed it. I traveled with the crew, did continuity scenes, little chats about EP, and the interviews in Italian.

RAMBLING AROUND POUND'S *Propertius*

1. Choate preparatory school is a well-known school in Connecticut. John F. Kennedy went there. The "honest sailor" sermon is familiar to older graduates of the school. Since Choate merged with the girls' school, Rosemary Hall, it's called Choate-Rosemary Hall.

2. The German publisher Mueller had a famous set of editions of the classics. Pound worked from this edition in doing his *Propertius*.

3. Robert Bridges (1844–1930) was an English poet who became the Poet Laureate in 1913. His most famous work is *The Testament of Beauty,* a long philosophical poem he published in 1929.

4. Zenos Metevsky, Pound's name for Sir Basil Zaharoff, the international dealer in armaments, appears in Canto 17.

5. Professor Davie's almost *ad hominem* review of Williams's *Collected Poems* in *The New Republic* for April 20, 1987 is, for me at least, painful reading.

6. "Loebing" refers to the Loeb Classical Library bilingual volumes in which many people, including myself, read the classics.

AN INTRODUCTION TO THE *Cantos*

1. This chapter was originally written for the *New York Times Book Review* to commemorate Ezra Pound's one hundredth birthday.

2. Pound attributes this definition to Agricola, however, Eva Hesse, Pound's German translator, has traced it back to the Latin rhetorician Quintilian (1st century, A.D.).

SOME VOICES FROM CANTO 74

1. The page references are to the current New Directions edition of the *Cantos*.

2. Louis Agassiz (1807–73) was a zoologist and geologist born in Switzerland who became a professor at Harvard in 1845. He was one of Pound's idols for his systematic thinking.

3. *Matthews' Chinese Dictionary* was one of the dictionaries Pound used for his translations.

4. The lovely tag for a girl, "dulce ridentem" (sweetly laughing), turns up also in Horace's "Integer Vitae." The lives of the two poets slightly overlapped, but it may simply have been a phrase in poetic parlance around Rome in those days.

5. See Ezra Pound: *Plays Modelled on the Noh*, edited by Donald C. Gallup, Toledo, Ohio, The Friends of the University of Toledo Libraries, 1987.

POUND'S ECONOMICS

1. Clifford Hugh Douglas (1879–1952) was an English engineer and social economist. He was the founder of the monetary reform movement of Social Credit. His books include *Social Credit*, *The Monopoly of Credit*, and *The Use of Money*.

E. P.: THE LIGHTER SIDE

1. Oliver St. John Gogarty, the poet, model for Buck Mulligan in Joyce's *Ulysses*, became a senator of Ireland in 1922.

CHRONOLOGY

The first section of this chronology, which he headed "autobiography," was written by Pound himself for inclusion in the New Directions' 1949 edition of his *Selected Poems*. Below the rule I have added further dates and information.

E.P.

Born, Hailey, Idaho, 30 Oct. 1885.
Educ. U. of Penn. and Hamilton. Ph.D. '05. M.A. '06.

Published. 1908. Venice; A Lume Spento.

1909, Mathews, London. Personae, Exultations.
Thereafter some 40 volumes, in London till 1910.

New York 1920–'30.

1930 onwards, with Faber, London, and in U.S.

1918 began investigation of causes of war, to oppose same. Lectured in the Università Bocconi, Milan, 1931, on Jefferson and Van Buren.

From 1932 continual polemic in two languages, moving from Social Credit to Gesellism.

Obtaining imprint in Italy of Social Credit and Gesellite doctrines, comparing them with Catholic canonist theory and local practice.

1939 first visit to U.S. since 1910 in endeavour to stave off war. D.Litt, honorary, from Hamilton.

1940 after continued opposition obtained permission to use Rome radio for personal propaganda in support of U.S. Constitution, continuing after America's official entry into the war only on condition that he should never be asked to say anything contrary to his conscience or contrary to his duties as an American Citizen. Which promise was faithfully observed by the Italian Government.

1940. Pound begins his broadcasts on Radio Rome. Indicted for treason in 1943.

1945. He gives himself up to the U.S. Army and is confined, at first in a cage, in the Disciplinary Training Center near Pisa. He has a nervous breakdown yet is able to write *The Pisan Cantos,* his finest work in the *Cantos.* He is flown to Washington, D.C. for trial. The jury at a sanity hearing in federal court finds him of unsound mind.

1946–58. He is sent to St. Elizabeths Hospital and remains there for twelve years as "a guest of the Government." While in St. Elizabeths, where he is kindly treated, Pound continues his work on the *Cantos,* translates the *Confucian Odes,* Sophocles' *Women of Trachis* and *Elektra,* and compiles the *Confucius to Cummings* poetry anthology. He is allowed visitors and conducts his own kind of academy from a bathchair on the lawn.

1949. Award of the Bollingen Prize for *The Pisan Cantos* arouses extensive controversy.

1951–53. Publication of Pound's translation of the *Analects* of Confucius.

1954. Publication of the *Literary Essays* with an introduction by T. S. Eliot.

1955. Publication of *Section: Rock-Drill* (Cantos 85–95).

1958. Under pressure from other writers, the indictment against Pound is dropped. He returns to Italy where he lives for three years at the castle of his daughter, Mary de Rachewiltz, near Merano.

1959. Publication of *Thrones* (Cantos 96–109).

1961. After an extended illness he moves to the home of his longtime friend Olga Rudge in Venice. He is no longer strong enough to do much work on the *Cantos.*

1968. Publication of the last *Drafts & Fragments* of the *Cantos.*

1969. Final visit to the United States.

1972. Pound dies in Venice on November 1 at the age of 87. He is buried in the island cemetery of San Michele.

ABC of Reading. A primer of literary values.

The Cantos.

The Classic Noh Theatre of Japan, twenty plays adapted by Pound from the notebooks of Ernest Fenollosa.

Collected Early Poems. All of the poems of the 1908–1912 period, including the
ones which Pound did not collect in *Personae*.

Confucius. Translations of *The Great Digest*, *The Unwobbling Pivot*, and the *Analects*.

Confucius to Cummings. The anthology of poetry from many languages which
Pound assembled while in St. Elizabeths Hospital with the help of Marcella
Spann.

Correspondence volumes:

Ezra Pound and Dorothy Shakespear [Pound's Wife], 1909–1914.

Pound/Ford. [Ford Madox Ford].

Pound/Joyce: Letters & Essays.

Pound/Lewis. [Wyndham Lewis].

Pound/Zukofsky. [Louis Zukofsky].

Ezra Pound and Music. Pound's writings on music.

Ezra Pound and the Visual Arts. Writings on art.

Gaudier-Brzeska. Pound's memoir of the sculptor Henri Gaudier-Brzeska.

Guide to Kulchur

Literary Essays

Love Poems of Ancient Egypt

Pavannes and Divagations. A collection of lighter pieces.

Personae. All of the major shorter poems.

Selected Cantos. Pound's own selection. Paperback.

Selected Letters, 1907–1941.

Selected Poems. Paperback.

Selected Prose, 1909–1965.

The Spirit of Romance. A survey of Romance literature.

Translations. Pound's versions of poems from many languages.

Women of Trachis. Pound's adaptation of the Sophocles play.

All of the above are published by New Directions, many in paperback.

Ezra Pound Speaking: Radio Speeches of World War II. Greenwood Press.

The Classic Anthology as Defined by Confucius. [The Confucian Odes]. Harvard University Press.

Jefferson and/or Mussolini. Liveright.

POUND AND PROVENÇAL

There are several scholarly books which will be of interest to readers who wish to study Pound's love affair with Provençal in greater detail: *Ezra Pound and the Troubador Tradition* by Stuart Y. McDougal (Princeton University Press, 1971); *Provence and Pound* by Peter Makin (University of California Press, 1978); Paul Blackburn's *Proensa* (University of California Press, 1978); Frederick Golden's *Lyrics of the Troubadors and Trouvères* (Anchor Books, 1973); and James J. Wilhelm's *Seven Troubadors* (Pennsylvania State University Press, 1970); and *Medieval Song* (G. Allen and Unwin, 1971). Chapter 3 of Wilhelm's *The Later Cantos of Ezra Pound* (Walker, 1977) lists all the appearances of Provençal material in the *Cantos*, along with many significant critical insights about it. Pound's translations of some of the *minnesingers*, the German troubadors, will be found in *Forked Branches: Translations of Medieval Poems* (Windhover Press, Iowa City, 1985).

A SELECTIVE BIBLIOGRAPHY ON
POUND'S ECONOMIC IDEAS

BOOKS BY EZRA POUND

ABC of Economics. London: Faber and Faber, 1933; now included in *Selected Prose*, New York, New Directions, 1973. This work should be the basic text, but it is written in a boring way — simplistic, repetitive, and at times over elaborated. Pound set out to write a primer and abandoned all his usual vitalities of personal style. Most of the short pieces on economic themes in part 6 of his *Selected Prose* (see below) are more lively and instructive on specific points. See, for example, "A Study of Relations and Gesell," pp. 272–82.

"Ezra Pound Speaking": Radio Speeches of World War II. Edited by Leonard W. Doob. Westport: Greenwood Press, 1978.

Guide to Kulchur. New York: New Directions, 1952. The *Guide* contains scattered discussions of economic themes.

Impact. Edited by Noel Stock. Chicago: Regnery, 1960. Except the brief article "Destruction by Taxation," most of the economic pieces in this collection are in *Selected Prose*.

The Money Pamphlets Series. In 1950 or 1951, Pound edited a series of pamphlets on economic subjects that were published by his disciple Peter Russell in London, using Pound's own texts. This entire series appears in *Selected Prose*.

The Selected Letters of Ezra Pound. Edited by D. D. Paige. New York: New Directions, 1971. The letters in this volume end at 1930 and occasionally include comments on economic themes.

Selected Prose, 1909–1965. Edited by William Cookson. New York: New Directions, 1973. Part 6, "Civilization, Money, and History," contains twenty-six important pieces, many of which deal at least marginally with economics (e.g., "ABC of Economics," "An Introduction to the Economic Nature of the United States," "Gold and Work, 1944," "Banks," "A Visiting Card," and "What Is Money For?").

SOURCE BOOKS WHICH POUND USED
IN DEVELOPING HIS ECONOMIC THEORIES

Adams, Brooks. *America's Economic Supremacy*. New York: Macmillan, 1900.

——. *The Law of Civilization and Decay*. New York: Macmillan, 1897.

——. *The New Empire*. New York: Macmillan, 1903.

Beard, Charles. *Economic Origins of Jeffersonian Democracy*. New York: Macmillan, 1936.

Benton, Thomas Hart. *Thirty Years' View*. 1854. 2d ed. New York: Appleton, 1856.

Breglia, Alberto. *L'Economia del Punto di Vista Monetario*. Rome: Dell'Ateneo, n.d.

Bukharin, N. *The Economic Theory of the Leisure Class*. London: Lawrence, 1927.

Butchart, Montgomery. *Money*. London: S. Nott, 1935.

——. *Tomorrow's Money*. London: S. Nott, 1936.

Del Mar, Alexander. *Ancient Britain Revisited*. New York: Cambridge Encyclopedia, 1889.

——. *A History of Monetary Crimes*. Moscow, Idaho: Clearwater Publishers, n.d.

——. *History of Monetary Systems*. 1895. Reprint. Orono, Maine: National Poetry Foundation, 1983.

——. *A History of Money in America*. New York: Cambridge Encyclopedia, 1889.

——. *The Middle Ages Revisited*. New York: Cambridge Encyclopedia, 1900.

——. *Money and Civilization*. London: G. Bell and Sons, 1886.

——. *Roman and Moslem Moneys*. Washington, D.C.: Square Dollar Series, 1955.

——. *The Science of Money*. London: G. Bell and Sons, 1885.

Dewey, Davis R. *Financial History of the United States*. New York: Longmans, 1939.

Douglas, C. H. *The Alberta Experiment*. London: Eyre and Spottiswoode, 1937.

——. *Credit-Power and Democracy*. London: C. Palmer, 1920.

——. *The Control and Distribution of Production*. London: C. Palmer, 1922.

——. *The Douglas Manual*. Edited by Philip Mairet. Toronto: C. M. Dent and Sons, 1934.

——. *Economic Democracy*. London: C. Palmer, 1920.

——. *The Monopoly of Credit*. London: Chapman and Hall, 1931.

——. *The Nature of Democracy*. London: S. Nott, 1934.

——. *Social Credit*. London: C. Palmer, 1924.

——. *The Use of Money*. New York: New Economics Group, 1934.

——. *Warning Democracy*. London: C. M. Grieve, 1931.

Fisher, Irving. *100% Money*. New York: Adelphi, 1935.

——. *Stabilized Money*. London: Allen and Unwin, 1935.

Freeman, Joseph and Scott Nearing. *Dollar Diplomacy*. New York: Viking, 1926.

Gesell, Silvio. *The Challenge of Economic Freedom*. San Antonio, n.d.

——. *The Natural Economic Order*. Translated by Philip Pye. 2 vol. San Antonio: Free Economy Publishing, 1934–36.

Hollis, Christopher. *The Two Nations*. London: G. Routledge and Sons, 1935.

——. *We Aren't So Dumb*. London: Longmans, 1937.

Kitson, Arthur. *A Scientific Solution to the Money Question*. Boston: Arena Publishing, 1895.

——. *Money Problems*. Stamford: Dooby, 1920.

Larranaga, P. J. *Gold, Glut, and Government*. London: Allen and Unwin, 1932.

Lenin, V. I. *Imperialism the Highest Stage of Capitalism*. New York: International, 1934.

——. *State and Revolution*. New York: International, 1935.

Lockhart, L. W. *World Economy*. London: Kegan Paul, 1931.

Mark, Jeffrey. *The Modern Idolatry*. London: Chatto & Windus, 1934.

Marx, Karl. *Value, Price, and Profit*. New York: International, 1935.

Mathews, Frederick. *The £ and the $ or Gold, Debts and Taxes*. Paris: Vendome, 1932.

Orage, A. R. *An Alphabet of Economics*. London: T. F. Unwin, 1917.

Overholser, Willis A. *A History of Money in the United States*. Libertyville, Illinois: Progress Publishing Concern, 1936.

Por, Odon. *Finanza Nuova*. Florence: Le Monnier, 1940.

——. *Italy's Policy of Social Economics, 1930–1940*. Translated by Ezra Pound. Bergamo, Italy: Istituto italiano d'arti grafiche, 1941.

Roover, Raymond. *The Medici Bank*. New York: NYU Press, 1948.

Salmasio, Claudio. *De Modo Usurarum*. Paris: Elzevir, 1639.

Soddy, Frederick. *The Role of Money*. London: G. Routledge and Sons, 1934.

——. *Wealth, Virtual Wealth, and Debt*. 2d ed. New York: Dutton, 1933.

Sorosina, Amedeo. *Il Banco Giro di Venezia*. Venice: Visenti, 1889.

——. (Monte dei Paschi). *Per il Terzo Centenario*. Siena: Lazzeri, 1925.

Van Buren, Martin. *The Autobiography of Martin Van Buren*. Edited by John C. Fitzpatrick. Washington: Government Printing Office, 1920.

Voorhis, Jerry. *Dollars and Sense*. Washington: Government Printing Office, 1938.

——. *Out of Debt, Out of Danger*. New York: Devin-Adair, 1943.

Warburg, James P. *The Money Muddle*. London: Routledge, 1934.

Wilson, Robert McNair. *The Mind of Napoleon: A Study of Napoleon, Mr. Roosevelt, and the Money Power*. London: G. Routledge and Sons, 1934.

Woodward, W. E. *A New American History*. New York: Farrar and Rinehart, 1936.

NOTE:

I am indebted to Tim Redman for many of the titles in this section. His catalog of Pound's annotated copies of certain books in his personal library at Brunnenburg, Yale, and the Humanities Research Center at the University of Texas will be found in Volume 15, Numbers 2 & 3 of *Paideuma*. This book list shows how much Pound studied to formulate his economic theories. JL

BOOKS ABOUT POUND'S ECONOMICS
AND RELATED SUBJECTS

Davis, Earl. *Vision Fugitive*. Lawrence: University Press of Kansas, 1968.

Hargrave, John. *Social Credit Clearly Explained*. London: SCP Publishing House, 1945.

Holter, Elizabeth Sage. *Social Credit*. London: S. Nott, 1934.

Kenner, Hugh. *The Pound Era*. Berkeley and Los Angeles: University of California Press, 1971.

Munson, Gorham. *Aladdin's Lamp*. New York: Creative Age Press, 1945.

INDEX

Fitzgerald, Robert, 91, 127
Fitzgerald, Zelda, 148
Flaubert, Gustave, 7, 55
Fleming, Rudd, 22, 44, 46–47
Flory, Wendy, 155
Ford, Charles Henri, 41
Ford, Ford Madox, 7, 39, 55, 58, 63,
    102, 149, 169
Four Pages, 24, 41
Fox, Douglas, 123, 125
French, William E., 41
Francis, Saint, 149
Freud, Sigmund, 151
Frobenius, Leo, 123–27
Frost, Robert, 26, 35

Gallinger Hospital, 21
Gallup, Donald, 56, 93, 148
Gaudier-Brzeska, Henri, 13, 16,
    35–36, 40, 94, 152–53
Gautier, Judith, 44
Gautier, Théophile, 50
George, Henry, 158–59
George V, King of England, 178
Gesell, Silvio, 12, 38, 107, 140,
    152–53, 158–60
Gibbon, Edward, 4
Gilbert, Dr. (Gallinger Hospital), 22
Ginsberg, Allen, 12
Giraut de Borneil, 88
Gnostics, 85
Goethe, Johann Wolfgang von, 140
Gordon, David, 25, 41, 128, 146
Gourmont, Remy de, 6
Gregory, Horace, 131
Grene, David, 91
Grover, Philip, 81
Guinizelli, Guido, 70

H. D. See Doolittle, Hilda
Hale, William G., 92, 101
Hammarskjöld, Dag, 25
Hargrave, John, 156
Harper's, 154
Harris, Joel Chandler, 121, 175
Hauge, Gabriel, 26
Heine, Heinrich, 140–42

Hemingway, Ernest, 4, 26, 148
    A Moveable Feast, 36
    In Our Time, 39
Henghes. See Klussmann
Henry II, King of England, 71
Herodotus, 6, 122–23, 166
Herter, Christian, 25
Hessler, L. Burton, 56
Hillyer, Robert, 92
Hollis, Christopher, 154
Holter, E. S., 155
Homer, 107, 127–28
Horton, David, 41
Hound & Horn, 3, 41
Hui (ruler of China), 168
Hyde, Lewis, 166

Innocent III, 85

Jackson, Andrew, 161
James, Henry, 7, 36, 55, 60–61
Janows, Jill, 51
Jebb, Sir Richard C., 47
Jefferson, Thomas, 20, 38, 107, 112,
    154, 161, 162, 166
Jenkyns, John, 119
John of the Cross, Saint, 149
Jonson, Ben, 144–45
Joyce, James, 3, 7, 18, 35, 40–42,
    55, 131, 149, 179
Juliana, Queen of Holland, 17–18
Jung, C. G., 125

Kasper, John, 25
Kavka, Jerome, 22, 179
Kazin, Alfred, 14, 165
Kenner, Hugh, 8, 25, 60, 96, 99,
    102, 120, 142, 155
Keynes, John Maynard, 156
King, Dr. (witness at Pound's sanity
    hearing), 22
Kirstein, Lincoln, 3, 41
Kitasono, Katue, 44
Kitson, Arthur, 154
Klussmann, Heinz Winterfeld, 13
Kretschmer, 77

A NOTE ON JAMES LAUGHLIN

At the age of twenty James Laughlin studied with Ezra Pound at the "Ezuversity" in Rapallo, Italy. Pound urged Laughlin to become a publisher, and the avant-garde press of New Directions was formed. New Directions has published twenty-six Pound books, all of them still in print. Further volumes of Pound's correspondence with other writers are to follow.

A friendship developed between poet and publisher that became an almost filial relationship. Laughlin visited Pound frequently over the years in Italy and during the twelve years when Pound was confined in St. Elizabeths Hospital in Washington, D.C. There were constant exchanges of letters. Thus Laughlin is able to give personal memories of "Ez as Wuz" and to report insights about Pound's work that came "from the horse's mouth."

In 1984 and 1986 Laughlin led seminars on Pound at Brown University. In 1985, the anniversary of Pound's birth, he was invited to speak at conferences at Yale and the Universities of Maine, Alabama, and San Jose State.

While most of the chapters in this book are lectures — or "conversations with students" as he prefers to call them — there are other features: a piece on the *Cantos* commissioned by the *New York Times Book Review*; a humorous treatment — Laughlin terms it a "rigolade" — of the *Homage to Sextus Propertius*, Pound's most engaging long poem; the text of a little known story written in 1907, "In the Water-Butt," with commentary; and a scenario for a classroom performance by students of original texts from nine languages that were in Pound's head when, with no books available, he wrote *The Pisan Cantos* from memory in the Army's Disciplinary Training Center near Pisa.

This book was designed by Tree Swenson.

The type is Palatino, set by Fjord Press Typography.

The book was printed and bound by Arcata Graphics.

PHOTO CREDITS : page 11, James Angleton; page 27, Ann Laughlin; page 31, Robert T. Chaffee; page 33, Ann Laughlin; page 40, Arnold Genthe; page 114, Vanni Scheiwiller; page 159, Olga Rudge; page 163, James Laughlin.

Front cover photo by Polly Forbes-Johnson.
Back cover photo by Ann Laughlin.